META-NARRATIVES:
Essays on
PHILOSOPHY *and*
SYMBOLISM

JAY DYER

META-NARRATIVES: ESSAYS ON PHILOSOPHY AND SYMBOLISM

Scripture taken from the King James Version of the Bible.

iUniverse books may be ordered through booksellers or by contacting:

iUniverse
1663 Liberty Drive
Bloomington, IN 47403
www.iuniverse.com
844-349-9409

Because of the dynamic nature of the Internet, any web addresses or links contained in this book may have changed since publication and may no longer be valid. The views expressed in this work are solely those of the author and do not necessarily reflect the views of the publisher, and the publisher hereby disclaims any responsibility for them.

Any people depicted in stock imagery provided by Getty Images are models, and such images are being used for illustrative purposes only.
Certain stock imagery © Getty Images.

ISBN: 978-1-6632-3998-3 (sc)
ISBN: 978-1-6632-3999-0 (e)

Library of Congress Control Number: 2022909195

Print information available on the last page.

iUniverse rev. date: 06/22/2022

CHAPTER 1

The Good of Metaphysics

The definition of metaphysics, despite what booksellers may offer in the way of do-it-yourself witchcraft manuals and stories of UFOs, is much different than any popular misconception of its meaning. For Aristotle, fourth-century BCE Greek philosopher, the starting point of wisdom, or philosophy, was metaphysics. Modernity, in its quest for self-destruction, has more or less rejected metaphysics. But metaphysics will never go away because metaphysics is reality itself— the study of the totality of *what is*. Metaphysics is the starting point in terms of actual foundations of knowledge and presupposition, yet it comes at the end of the process of pedagogy, as it is the highest science. Nowadays, aside from certain continental philosophers who follow in the train of genius writers like nineteenth/twentieth-century German philosopher mathematician Edmund Husserl, *theoria* and metaphysics have been jettisoned for pragmatism, postmodernism, and other forms of self-destructive prattle. And over the length of centuries in the West, there's been no lack of contributors to this gradual decline.[1]

Unfortunately, certain basic flaws in Aristotle's own position led to that decline, particularly his adoption of empiricism. Aristotle cut the world off from the possibility of any other world or reality or dimension, and while it took a millennium or two, this ultimately resulted in materialism, positivism, and finally the negation of all

1

meaning and purpose. In fact, that last notion was crucial for early moderns like Francis Bacon who, as a philosopher in the seventeenth century, did have legitimate disagreements with Aristotle. Aristotle had adopted several ideas about the natural world from tradition; for example, the heavens are perfectly unchanged, static realities, and rocks have an essential quality of "going downward." Bacon rightly laughed at this, but what Bacon didn't foresee was that tossing out Aristotle's final cause, or telos, would result in the total collapse of philosophy.

The place of Dominican priest and philosopher Thomas Aquinas in the thirteenth century can also not be forgotten on this slope of decline. Aquinas followed suit with an Aristotelian-Platonic synthesis (so he thought), which placed human reasoning on an independent basis that never touched the divine, since the absolutely simple divine essence, within which the divine archetypes upon which even "natural" reasoning was based, were never accessed by the minds of humanity in this life. Aquinas upheld this notion due to his idea of simplicity: divinity, which is also the ground of human knowledge, never interacts with or connects to the abstracted phantasms of a person's mind, since the exemplars themselves are in the divine essence, a first cause that is only able to reveal itself by created effects in this life. Bacon departed from these ideas and turned to a more consistent (so he thought) empiricism.

We don't observe a telos, or purpose. We observe cause and effect, and from a human vantage point. But this is a double-edged sword: If things don't have any purpose, essence, or meaning outside of the arbitrary "meaning" individual humans ascribe to them, then meaning doesn't inhere over time, and we end up with identity problems. David Hume, eighteenth-century Scottish Enlightenment philosopher, elucidated about this over time. Certainly Bacon still thought there was a deity and meaning in the world, but he set in motion the train of (flawed) reasoning that would ultimately dispose of any objective meaning. If we adopt Bacon's more consistent Thomistic, more consistent Aristotelian empiricism, then give it time, we shall end up with Hume's radical skepticism. And radical skepticism led moderns to adopt bizarre, destructive philosophies like nihilism, postmodernism, and other emanations of the humanist faith. Immanuel Kant, eighteenth-century German philosopher, was thus right to seek an answer to Hume in transcendental categories because that signified a return to the crucial area of *a priori* notions, about which Plato was right and Aristotle was wrong (though Aristotle was right about quite a lot).

For Kant, the solution was to reconcile how there could be a synthetic a priori claim that was true: how can we make an a priori claim about all experience? Kant, following the Aristotelian notion of transcendental arguments, correctly listed preconditional necessary categories that were presupposed in any human experience of cognition. However, Kant traveled the road of folly by still ascribing to empiricism, and in so doing, his categories never touched the objective, external world. Kant could never know if any of his claims and arguments were actually true of the noumenal world, and so he stated they were true only of the phenomena of experience as they appeared. And from there, as a rationalist, he tacked on all kinds of other ideas that would only further the cause of destroying what was one of the greatest insights in the history of philosophy—preconditional categories of experience proven by indirect transcendental argumentation.

The solution to this imagined dilemma is rather simple: toss out the illusory divide between the phenomenal and noumenal and hold to a direct experience of the world—to which the transcendental categories do indeed apply—and explain the objective world to which all people are party. This approach not only works; it makes sense, and it explains how we do things like see, interpret, walk, analyze, build rockets, form sentences, and so forth. Brilliant philosophers like twentieth-century philosopher P. F. Strawson have carried on this monumental work of real philosophy in transcendental arguments, venturing into the realm that most obviously demonstrates this—linguistics. For a person to make a single sentence presupposes an entire world structured in a certain way; this is the salvation and continuation of real philosophy, while the prophets of relativism and postmodern fantasists will be left in the dust.

So we can salute Aristotle in his primacy of metaphysics and be simultaneously saddened in his acceptance of the nascent empiricism that would be the death of the West, a process ending in all-corroding relativism. It may have taken a few thousand years to realize the full implications of the supposedly neutral "scientific method" unto civilization's collapse, and if there is to be science any longer, it must recognize that theoria and philosophy are vitally necessary. Naturally, it is a problem not so much of intellect as of the proud human psyche in convincing our fellows to even understand what transcendental arguments are and why they are relevant.

Questions such as these should appeal to Gödelian mathematical types, who are often far better equipped to tackle these issues than so-called "philosophers" of our modern universities, intellectual harlequins who are in truth nothing other than the sophists Plato and Aristotle once conquered. It's no accident that the ancient sophists are an unknown rabble aside from one or two obscure names. Thousands of years later, the world is still blessed to know who Plato and Aristotle are. The sooner the modern sophists pass out of existence, the better. Let us hail a return to Aristotle and logic purged of its errors—a return to sound reasoning—to the trivium and quadrivium, and to the transcendent and the sacral.

Symbolic and Numerological Elements in Achilles' Shield and Plato's Timaeus

The epic Greek poem, *liad*, written by Homer probably in the eighth century BCE, is a foundational work of Western civilization, and one of its most famous sections is the book that deals with the forging of the shield for the great warrior Achilles by the god of metallurgy, Hephaestus. While the story of the forging of the shield occupies a lengthy book, this book will examine the beginning of Hephaestus's work, highlighting the numerology, shape, and imagery from lines 560–600. In this section, it is apparent that the shield functions not merely as a defensive piece, but as a symbolic construct for the Greek worldview itself.

At the imploring of Thetis, mother of Achilles, Hephaestus began crafting a shield that "... any man in the world of men will marvel at through all the years to come—whoever sees its splendor" (ll. 545–6), cluing the hearer into the special, surreal nature of this armor.[2] In other words, this is not common armor, but in fact will become a microcosm display of the totality of the Greek worldview itself. It is significant to note that the image chosen for the Greek world is a circular shield (about which shape more will be said later) and that what first appears is the defensive nature of the symbol. Homer could have chosen a sword with engravings or a spear, but instead chose a defensive article, intending the reader to see the proper place of warfare as a necessary evil in this life. Indeed, the *Iliad* itself famously portrays the strife and misery caused by warfare. Thus, Homer would have hearers of his epic understand that true wisdom sees that warfare should have a defensive, balancing role in the protection and maintenance of civilized order.

Homer continued:

And first Hephaestus makes a great and massive shield,

blazoning well-wrought emblems across its surface,

raising a rim around it, glittering, triple-ply,

with a silver shield-strap run from edge to edge

and five layers of metal to build the shield itself,

and across a vast expanse with all his craft and
cunning

the god creates a world of gorgeous immortal work.[3]

Translator Fagles chose to use the word *world*, indicating that
the shield's purpose is not merely as a weapon for Achilles, but as
a microcosm image of the entire Greek worldview. It has, in effect,
the function of a Creation account. The shield itself is possibly
even a mnemonic device through which the oral tradition of the
Greek account of Creation might possibly be recalled; it may as well
function as a memory device for the Greek orator reciting the story.
Critic James M. Redfield explains of this totality world notion:

> The wider world appears in the minds of the
> characters, who often speak of a time of peace or
> of a place at peace. It appears also in the mind of
> the poet, particularly in the similes. Each simile
> is a kind of window through which we glimpse a
> world beyond the battlefield of Troy. Through the
> device of the simile, the wider world is included in
> the narrower. Through the similes the battlefield
> is located within the wider world and, at the same
> time, resembles all the various aspects of the wider
> world, so that the parts recapitulate the whole.[4]

This concept of the wider macrocosm being encapsulated in
the smaller microcosm is profuse in the Greek tradition. A later
example from Plato's *Timaeus* includes the idea of the universe as
a whole being in a kind of shape like a man, or the *macroprosopus*.
Plato described the gods as creating the universe as a sphere, like
a human head, wherein reason governs the motions of the body,
corresponding to the universal reason which governs the spherical
universe itself.[5]

The triplicity mentioned is also relevant inasmuch as numbers, in Greek culture, have a semidivine status. It is from Pythagoras, of course, that we have the tradition of the divinity and esoteric character of numbers, but this symbolism also comes forth in Homer, for whom the construction of the three-ply shield corresponds to the familiar three-tiered world with the perfect spherical heavens at the top, the earth beneath the heavens, and then the underworld beneath the earth. The shield itself does not present this as the meaning, but as a Greek, he would have seen the world as stacked in this way. The use of three, however, also occurs in Plato's Creation account in which the eternal god creates the world through the demiurge, and since a dyad cannot stand alone, must then reciprocate itself to the god, producing a third principle, divine sophia, which governs the world.[6]

Strikingly, while Plato linked this principle of sophia, or divine wisdom, with Athena, after mentioning the three-ply nature of the shield, Homer proceeded to mention the two gods whose images adorn the shield: Ares and Pallas.[7] Dialectical process was a central notion to the Greeks, whose culture was itself based around oral rhetorical dialectics. Thus, the dialectical balance of war and wisdom constantly displayed in the *Iliad* as Athena fought for the Greeks and Ares for the Trojans displayed the dialectical balance of forces in the Greek tradition itself. In fact, as Homer's description moved on, he told of two cites, one at peace and one at war—again, showing the dialectical balance. For the Greek mind, the number two was a signifier of opposition and duality, overcome only by the dialectical synthesis of the triad. As Plato explained: "But two things cannot be put together without a third."[8]

It is also worth noting that Hephaestus, Greek god of artisans, took the raw metallic ore and crafted a balanced, ordered shield from the chaos of the fire and smelting process, imposing order out of chaos, just as Plato's *Timaeus* presented the eternal god shaping order out of chaos. The shield went on to demonstrate the ordered, cyclical progression of the seasons, a circular dance, as well as the shield itself being circular. This is crucial to the Greek mind inasmuch as the circle was seen as a perfect image of the divine, being itself never ending. The Greek view of time was cyclical, not linear, and was bound up with the notion of a circular universe. Plato echoed the shield imagery when he wrote of the universe itself: "For as the universe is in the form of a sphere, all the extremities being equidistant from the center, are equally extremities, and the center, which is equidistant from them, is equally to be regarded as the opposite of them all."[9]

It is apparent, then, that Homer imagined the Greek world in the shield of Achilles, which functioned as a microcosm of the totality of macrocosm; in this case, a restatement of a kind of Greek Creation account in which a complex yet mystical mathematical order was imposed on the chaos of raw substance: in Homer, Hephaestus on the shield; in Plato, the god upon the raw chaos of matter. For the Greeks, then, the imposition of order demanded a civilized society that mirrored the order found within the eternal spheres where the celestial gods resided. It was on Earth where the battles of gods and men were fought, and where the dialectical dyad was balanced and transcended, yet not without the heavenly order that descended from the divine.

The famed shield of Achilles is a mysterious, yet well-known chapter from Homer's classic, the *Iliad*. Within the chapter is contained an entire microcosmic representation of the Greek worldview replete with unique numerological significations as well as other symbolic motifs intended to convey, through imagery, an entire hierarchical cosmology. The purpose of this book will be to examine the specific numbers and symbols used and to compare them with other roughly contemporary traditions, such as Plato's cosmological explanations. The intent is to achieve a greater understanding of the Greek mind as it viewed the totality of reality, comparing earlier mythological oral poetry with its later offspring, philosophy itself.[10]

The shield of Achilles and the rest of his armor embodied the Greek conception of the hero as intimately and magically connected to his armor. The Greek warrior sought glory first and foremost, or timé, and the path to glory was one of successful warfare. Literary critic Kenneth John Atchity explained, "Achilles is the epitome of Iliadic man. The two artifacts which belong uniquely to him, Hephaestos' shield and Peleus' spear define not only the identity of Achilles, but also the essence of human nature as Homer conceives of it."[11] As is evident in Homer, the individualistic focus of the Greeks upon the singular hero is unique. Historian Michael Grant commened:

> With lively, yet disengaged comprehension, each personage is depicted as a distinct individual [in the *Iliad*]. The most arresting is Achilles, who possesses in extreme degree all the virtues and faults of the Homeric hero, and almost completely embodies the heroic code of honor ... [Homer] dedicated his entire existence, with all the aid that his birth and wealth and physical prowess could afford him, to an unceasing, violently competitive, vengeful struggle to win applause ...[12]

Undoubtedly, in such a society, the warrior's armor and weaponry would be bound up with his very existence and survival. It is fitting, then, that the shield was the instrument chosen by Homer to embody the microcosm of the Greek worldview. In fact, much more than just the shield itself is relevant: the deities involved in which actions and artifacts are also significant as well as Achilles himself being an incarnation of the ancient Grecian culture as will be shown. The Creation of the shield arises from Achilles's divine mother, Thetis, who interceded on his behalf with the Olympian artificer and god of the underworld, Hephaestos. Thetis was a sea goddess who gave birth to Achilles through union with a mortal. Achilles occupied the demigod status as a middle ground between the world of the mortals and that of the immortal gods. He was not fully divine, but was more closely attuned to the realm of the gods than most humans. Homer even gave an early image of his apotheosis prior to the forging of the shield:

> And Iris racing the wind went veering off
>
> as Achilles, Zeus' favorite fighter, rose up now
>
> and over his shoulder Pallas slung the shield,
>
> the tremendous storm-shield with all its tassles flaring—
>
> and crowning his head the goddess swept a golden cloud and from it she lit a fire to blaze across the field …
>
> so now from Achilles' head the blaze shot up the sky …
>
> and charioteers were struck dumb when they saw that fire,
>
> relentless, terrible, burst from proud-hearted Achilles' head,
>
> blazing as fiery-eyed Athena fueled the flames.[13]

Pallas Athena was the embodiment of the principle of wisdom, or sophia, and was the patron deity of Athens itself.[14] The Greeks, prizing wisdom, here gave Achilles the embodiment of divine wisdom by deifying him through the fire of Athena. Achilles was also preferred by Zeus as his favorite fighter. Zeus here embodied the principle of timé, in that he rewarded the outcome of warfare with apotheosis through his daughter, Athena, the virgin emanation from his head.[15] The appearance of Zeus and Athena resulted in the imposition of order upon the chaos of the battlefield. This will become an important theme as the chapter progresses. Relevant also is the deification of Achilles's head, as opposed to his hands or a weapon. Athena, embodying wisdom and emanating from Zeus's head, would naturally be associated with Achilles's head, the seat of humanly wisdom and intelligence.

In Plato's *Timaeus*, which is a cosmology of the universe purportedly descending through a hermetic tradition from the priests of Egypt, there is an interesting parallel.[16] First, Plato wrote that Athena was the same deity the Egyptians identified as Nieth, and Athena granted to the people of Greece her patronage and special blessing since they were to be the wisest.[17] The republic was a polis modeled after Atlantis, which was patterned like the ideal realm of the forms.[18] The reason this is crucial is that Plato saw the entire visible sphere as a vastly organized hierarchy brought into visible form out of chaos. In other words, order out of chaos.[19] Indeed, for Plato, the entire universe had a built-in hierarchical structure that was to be followed rigorously in all areas of life. The polis was to be organized after the image of a man who was governed by reason, which mirrors the celestial hierarchy, which in turn reflects the chain of being, as is the entire argument of Plato's Socratic dialogue, *The Republic*.

Achilles thus embodied the Athenian warrior ruled and governed by wisdom, ideally, though Achilles was still mortal and fatally flawed, giving in to rage. His duty was to bring order out of chaos and incarnate the Greek ideals, and it was his shield that demonstrated precisely this. Homer wrote:

And first Hephaestus makes a great and massive shield,

blazoning well-wrought emblems across its surface,

raising a rim around it, glittering, triple-ply,

with a silver shield-strap run from edge to edge

and five layers of metal to build the shield itself,

and across a vast expanse with all his craft and
cunning

the god creates a world of gorgeous immortal work.[20]

The shield was massive, firstly, which is a clue to the surreal and
fantastical nature of the object. It was not an actual shield for battle;
rather, it was a special, magical device.[21] There were many images on
its surface, and was circular with a triple-ply construct. The shield
functioned as a cosmology, or Creation account, much like Plato's
Timaeus. Fagles uses the word *world* to describe the work. Critic
James M. Redfield explains of this totality world notion:

> The wider world appears in the minds of the
> characters, who often speak of a time of peace or
> of a place at peace. It appears also in the mind of
> the poet, particularly in the similes. Each simile
> is a kind of window through which we glimpse a
> world beyond the battlefield of Troy. Through the
> device of the simile, the wider world is included in
> the narrower. Through the similes the battlefield
> is located within the wider world and, at the same
> time, resembles all the various aspects of the wider
> world, so that the parts recapitulate the whole.[22]

A wider macrocosm being encapsulated in the smaller microcosm
was profuse in the Greek tradition. A later example from Plato's

Timaeus includes the idea of the universe as a whole being in a kind of shape like a man, or the macroprosopus. Plato wrote:

> First, then, the gods, imitating the spherical shape of the universe, enclosed the two divine courses in a spherical body, that, namely, which we now term the head, being the most divine part of us and the lord of all that is in us: to this the gods, when they put together the body, gave all the other members to be servants, considering that it partook of every sort of motion. In order then that it might not tumble about among the high and deep places of the earth, but might be able to get over the one and out of the other, they provided the body to be its vehicle and means of locomotion; which consequently had length and was furnished with four limbs extended and flexible; these God contrived to be instruments of locomotion with which it might take hold and find support, and so be able to pass through all places, carrying on high the dwelling-place of the most sacred and divine part of us.[23]

Plato described the gods as creating the universe as a sphere, like a human head, wherein reason governed the motions of the body corresponding to the universal reason that governs the spherical universe itself. Reason was to govern the passions as in a chariot, emblematic of the divine light or Athena's wisdom that enlightened Achilles.

However, most prominent was the circular and/or spherical imagery. The shield's circularity provided an excellent conduit for explicating the importance of the circle to the Greek. For Plato, the circle was by nature the most perfect of mathematical symbols. In fact, the entire universe, created ideally perfect but the highest deity, was a spherical living being. It was one of the earliest usages of the "ouroboros," the symbol of the serpent devouring its own tail. Plato explained the Egyptian doctrine he received as follows:

> Wherefore he made the world in the form of a globe, round as from a lathe, having its extremes in every direction equidistant from the center, the most perfect and the most like itself of all figures; for he considered that the like is infinitely fairer than the unlike. This he finished off, making the surface smooth all round for many reasons; in the first place, because the living being had no need of eyes when there was nothing remaining outside him to be seen; nor of ears when there was nothing to be heard; and there was no surrounding atmosphere to be breathed; nor would there have been any use of organs by the help of which he might receive his food or get rid of what he had already digested, since there was nothing which went from him or came into him: for there was nothing beside him. Of design he was created thus, his own waste providing his own food, and all that he did or suffered taking place in and by himself. For the Creator conceived that a being which was self-sufficient would be far more excellent than one which lacked anything; and, as he had no need to take anything or defend himself against any one, the Creator did not think it necessary to bestow upon him hands: nor had he any need of feet, nor of the whole apparatus of walking; but the movement suited to his spherical form was assigned to him, being of all the seven that which is most appropriate to mind and intelligence; and he was made to move in the same manner and on the same spot, within his own limits revolving in a circle. All the other six motions were taken away

from him, and he was made not to partake of their deviations. And as this circular movement required no feet, the universe was created without legs and without feet.[24]

The creator created a perfectly circular Creation, just as the shield embodied. The circularity demonstrated a cyclical view of history common to the Greeks as opposed to a linear conception of time. Plato saw the universe as eternally providing for itself with no beginning or end. The snake imagery was useful inasmuch as the snake had no need for hands or feet, and had no need for spatial alteration. However, we are also told that the shield had an element of triplicity. This corresponds to the cross section view of the cosmos viewed from one perspective in which the scheme looks something like this:

———————————

Olympian heavenly gods

———————————

Mortals

———————————

Underworld

———————————

The clear meaning was not presented by the shield, but to the Greek, it would have been viewed as structured in this manner. The use of three also ocurred in Plato's *Timaeus* in which the eternal god created the living universe through a secondary demiurge, and since a dyad cannot stand alone according to his Pythagorean presuppositions, the first principle must then reciprocate itself to the creator god, producing a third principle, divine sophia, which governed the world. He writes:

> Now that which is created is of necessity corporeal, and also visible and tangible. And nothing is visible where there is no fire, or tangible which has no solidity, and nothing is solid without earth. Wherefore also God in the beginning of Creation made the body of the universe to consist of fire and earth. But two things cannot be rightly put together without a third; there must be some bond of union between them. And the fairest bond is that which makes the most complete fusion of itself and the things which it combines; and proportion is best adapted to effect such a union. For whenever in any three numbers, whether cube or square, there is a mean, which is to the last term what the first term is to it; and again, when the mean is to the first term as the last term is to the mean—then the mean becoming first and last, and the first and last both becoming means, they will all of them of necessity come to be the same, and having become the same with one another will be all one.[25]

This Creation scheme is very close to the imagery of the shield, especially its aspect of relating and encompassing all things. For the Platonist or the ancient Greek, all of life had meaning. Every aspect of life, whether it was the four seasons, warfare, the gods, or dance, was a vital part of a lived liturgy. Hephaestos continued the shield forging, using the blazing sun, the moon, and several constellations that all proceed in a similar circular fashion as before.[26] This again highlights the interconnectedness of all things for the Greeks. The stars as well as the planets had their place in the rounded heavens as the planets made their courses through the various zodiacal houses. Plato, too, included this astrological element in his system after discussing the planets:

> Thus he spake, and once more into the cup in which he had previously mingled the soul of the universe he poured the remains of the elements, and mingled them in much the same manner; they were not, however, pure as before, but diluted to the second and third degree. And having made it he divided the whole mixture into souls equal in number to the stars, and assigned each soul to a star; and having there placed them as in a chariot, he showed them the nature of the universe, and declared to them the laws of destiny, according to which their first birth would be one and the same for all ...[27]

This is the source of his famous transmigration of souls, or reincarnation, doctrine. The primitive Grecian of Homer's day would also have been at home with astrology, which is why it was given a prominent place on the shield. That one's fate was a determining factor in one's destiny was a common belief in the ancient world. The feeling of existence being determined by forces outside the individual's control gave rise to the religious fetish of deities associated with different constellations who controlled these events according to the "law of destiny" I have mentioned.

Next, the shield showed two cites. One was at war, and the other was at peace. And there were young men dancing while people in a law court decided a case in a "sacred circle."[28] Circular imagery was again prominent. Literary critic Laura Jepsen accurately explained the meaning here while discussing the anthropocentric focus of the Greeks:

> A glance at the circular motif reveals its import in pagan iconography. In the Iliad the "sacred circle" is represented by Achilles' shield, where around the rim flows the ocean embracing the world of Homeric civilization ... To the early Greek, the sanctity of the circle was expressed by the orchestra, the circular dancing place for worshippers celebrating the ritual around the altar of the god of wine, Dionysius, in whose honor tragedy traditionally originated.
>
> The author of comedy—if we can trust the brilliant discourse assigned by Plato to Aristophanes in Symposium—we are indebted to the explanation of Love by attributing the origin to primeval cosmic circle-men ... each human being was originally a whole with back and flanks rounded to form a circle ... They were akin to circular celestial bodies.[29]

Recall again Plato's "ouroboros." Since the heavens were closer to the gods and the ideal forms, it stands to reason that the true, ideal forms the original men created in and by "love" would have been spherical entities. Anything less than a perfect sphere would have been imperfect and unworthy of the creator according to the Platonic scheme. Aristophanes continued to argue that beings that existed in the present stage were partial by nature and always seeking wholeness; he claimed that the original beings were hermaphrodites.[30]

Redfield elucidates the use of the circles and the shield's literary function:

> The shield is intended as a systematic image of the wider world outside the Iliad. The patterns which emerge unreflectively in the similes have here been reflected upon and set into coherence. Yet this

very difference makes the shield a kind of master simile; the pattern of the shield can instruct us in our reading of the similes—remembering that our fundamental purpose is to grasp the Homeric understanding of the place of man in nature ... [N]ature is presented as stormy, violent, and dangerous; the weather similes are thus linked to the ocean similes ... Nature is hostile to man. The similes are linked to the shield—the ocean and shore similes being linked, obviously, to the outer rim, the weather similes to the center, through the link between stars and weather through the double role of Zeus as sender of meteorological signs and contriver of the weather.[31]

The world was being set into a pattern of coherence that was consonant with the Platonic doctrine that all reality was a vastly structured grid of forms, all measured and organized according to the Pythagorean principle of mathematics and having a divine status. For Plato, numbers and geometrical forms were the principal means to knowing the minds of the gods. When describing the nature of the bodies in the created visible universe, Plato said:

But three of them can be thus resolved and compounded, for they all spring from one, and when the greater bodies are broken up, many small bodies will spring up out of them and take their own proper figures; or, again, when many small bodies are dissolved into their triangles, if they become one, they will form one large mass of another kind. So much for their passage into one another. I have now to speak of their several kinds, and show out of what combinations of numbers each of them was formed.[32]

It is worth stressing the highly unique and all-encompassing scope Plato conceived that numbers had in describing the essence of true reality, which is the divine forms. Numbers constituted a kind of mystical go-between from our world to the ideal world. Twentieth-century Plato scholar G. M. Grube wrote:

> For the Platonic [thinker] number is the Idea of Good, or at any rate one aspect of the supreme Idea, mythically represented. Objectively considered the laws of the universe and the Ideas are mathematical. The conglomeration of elements which is a man, just as the movements of the stars, can be expressed as mathematical formulae. Time, space, sound are all mathematical from one point of view, and the purpose or supreme law of the universe can (or so Plato thought) be expressed in terms of numbers.[33]

This fits well with the numerical imagery of the shield, which used the numbers three and four as well as infinity (circularity). The infinite potentiality of numbers is partly what gave numbers such a mystique for the Pythagoreans, and certainly Plato inherited this idea.

It is also interesting to consider that the shield appears to involve an early form of taxonomic classification and ordering of different aspects of the Greek worldview. In other words, as well as being an oral myth, it also seems to have functioned as an early classification method. Plato saw dividing things according to such classifications as a logical process proper to the philosopher. This is what he attempted to do in a somewhat loose fashion in *Timaeus*, but interestingly, this was actually done more consistently by his student, Aristotle, whose scientific taxonomy we still use today. Grube explains:

> [T]he proper method of scientific discourse is said to be a right classification of things into classes

each of which corresponds to an Idea in nature, a process which is compared to dissection along the lines of joints. This logical method, here explained for the first time [in the *Phaedo*], consists then in dividing things into natural classes according to their common characteristics which correspond to the universal Forms. Men who can do this are dialecticians: they unite scattered things under one idea by means of division and synthesis.[34]

Nature thus presented apparent patterns and forms in the midst of its chaos. The gods appeared to act haphazardly, yet also in an ordered fashion. The Greeks' attempt to systematize their worldview thus conformed to the pattern they presupposed in their classification scheme itself. Thus, whether it is the gods ruling and embodying brute nature, or the flux of this lesser Creation that had slipped away from the realm of the ideal forms somehow, both presentations see an underlying ordering of the totality of reality according to mathematical and taxonomic actualities.

Twentieth-century Greek critic André Michalopoulos is correct when he refers to this as a "typical piece of unconscious background" (citing another commentator):

It gives us a picture of Greek life which must be natural since neither dramatic nor religious motives interfere to distort it. The writer is clearly describing a round shield with concentric zones of ornament such as are found on Phoenician bowls of later date ... To this day you may see the peasants of Greece dancing in rings and lines, with agile acrobats to lead them, just as they danced on the shield of Achilles. History goes on its pompous way, leaving the peasant unaltered and country life unchanged.

Indeed, we have a view of Greek life and thought that remained very much the same in Plato's day (fifth century BCE) as it was in Homer's (eighth century BCE), and Plato embodied the next step in the development of a more scientific and rationalist approach to the nature of reality over the more mythic and overtly religious character of Homer's tragedy as embodied on the shield and in Achilles himself. With Plato, the new hero became the philosopher king skilled at dialectics and the mathematical Pythagorean mysteries. No longer was the ideal man a warrior; rather, he was a thinker. However, both were ideally governed by the love of wisdom.

Notes:

1   Homer, *Iliad,* trans. Robert Fagles (New York: Pengiun Books, 1990), 482.
2   Ibid., 483.
3   Ibid., 558–64
4   James M. Redfield, *Nature and Culture in the Iliad* (Chicago: University of Chicago Press, 1979), 186.
5   Plato, *Timaeus*, ed. Edith Hamilton and Huntingdon Cairns (New Jersey: Princeton University Press, 1961), 1173. (See sections 43–44.)
6   Ibid., sections 30–32.
7   Homer, *Iliad,* 484. (l. 601).
8   Plato, *Timaeus,* section 31e.
9   Ibid., section 62e.
10
11
12
13 (ll. 234-62)
14
15
16
17
18
19
20 (ll. 558-64)

21
22
23
24
25
26
27
28
29
30
31
32
33
34

CHAPTER 2

Plato's Phaedo: *Dialectics and Logos*

Phaedo, the dialogue of Plato that concerns the final words of Socrates, is both profound and prone to strike the reader as bizarre and mysterious. The discussion revolves around a proposal by Socrates's associates to defend his views of the afterlife and the immortality of the soul, followed by a counter argument by a Pythagorean and a final rebuttal by Socrates before the recounting of his death by drinking hemlock. The work constitutes one of Plato's most notable dialogues: The influence of *Phaedo* on subsequent Western thought is clearly tremendous. And it's worth returning to after the undergrad days of philosophy 101 when one might have read a selection and hit the highlights of the doctrine of forms and immortality of the soul. In this book, we will investigate the epistemological, metaphysical, and esoteric teachings sprinkled along the way as well as problematic areas.

Early in the dialogue, Socrates mentioned his desire to practice the "arts" based on a recurring dream he has had. In response to queries about this, Socrates told his friends that philosophy was the greatest of the arts based on his attempt to create an Aesop-like fable of his own about the duality involved in pleasure and pain. The dialogue is also littered with references to initiation into the mysteries, the allegorical understanding given in religious initiations, and the idea that the initiates of the mysteries were prepared for journeys of the dead undertaken in the afterlife. Pleasure, he argued, is dialectically tied to pain, and both tend to ever bring their opposite. In this life, our attachment to bodily pleasure and passion thus becomes a hindrance that wears down the lofty, immortal nature of the soul. The allegorical meaning of the rites of the mysteries is therefore the philosophical understanding of how to live well so that, in the next life, we can pass on to blissful Valhalla. However, Socrates did not entirely spiritualize or allegorize the rites of the gods—he followed them in both senses.

The references to the mysteries and the rites of religion is curious, given the standard, secular version of this topic in academic settings, which generally focuses on a cursory overview and discards any esoteric ideas in the dialogues. Marxist, feminist, and statist education in our day is universally programmed to read all great works as externally imposed class and gender warfare diatribes that subvert everything wholesome and wondrous that might exist within them. And should you happen upon a male professor who isn't a feminist/Marxist, you likely found he was an atheist materialist who scoffed at anything in the work beyond his feeble grasp. Contrary to these sophistical losers, *Phaedo* is a religious treatise about initiatic knowledge through revelation. While all of these theses and ideas are not what I would recommend, *Phaedo* is a perennialist document and not a secular one.

For Plato and Socrates, the philosopher is one who lives according to virtue and reason, cultivating the pleasures of the soul and intellect and not the pleasures and passions of the baser desires of the body. The key to this path is grasping first that there are absolutes—absolute truth, goodness, beauty, and other aspects of life. These are universal forms that are recollected from our past lives and ultimately harken back to the One, or the monad, from which all things mysteriously emanated. We, as humans, "see" truly through the soul, and seeing with this higher, awakened eyesight allows us to peer into the higher realm of existence where truth is eternal, not subject to the chaotic flux and temporal finitude and change of this life. Antimaterial and, anachronistically, *gnostic* elements emerge here. And, later, Christian theology, for example, would connect gnostic movements to Platonism. One thinks of Origen's debates with Celsus, for example, or Augustine and Porphyry, and in both of those cases, Augustine and Origen unfortunately share too many of Platonism's presuppositions. Regardless, the antiphysical stance of Platonism actually demonstrates origins in much older traditions of the Far East. As the *Timaeus* recounts, the "mysteries" of Pythagoreanism and Platonism are those of Egypt.

Just as Augustine can be subjected to analogous criticism, the clear influence of Platonic errors is evident from *Phaedo*. The ascetic tendency to "despise the body" is present, also hearkening to older, ascetic traditions found in religions like Hinduism, so we are again presented with a perennial tradition at work here that is based on syncretic principles. The soul "sees" through the awakening of the philosophical sense as the soul wanders through the mirror reflections and copies of things (the particulars) on the way back to the One (the universals and the monad), and then engages in the cyclical process again; indeed, Socrates gave a detailed account of how the transmigration of souls takes place. The unfortunate and central place of Western dialectics is given primacy here where the eternal realm of unchanging forms is set over against the temporal realm of illusory reality. Ancient Far Eastern ideas of *maya* and empirical "reality" as unreality and deception are clearly present, and along with the transmigration of souls, these ridiculous doctrines should be dropped, based as they are on pagan conceptions of cyclical time and the chain of being wherein God, forms, humanity, and matter, are all placed at different levels on the same continuum of being. All based on≠≠ the presupposition of dialectics raised to a status of ultimate metaphysical principle, contraries, and oppositions found in nature are not transcended by setting these forces in eternal dualistic opposition.

In this scheme, death is on the same continuum as life, as a natural process, and time is illusory. The central absurdity here is that, if life is illusory, then the realization of life is illusory, as well. In other words, a presuppositional critique of the faulty metaphysical assumptions of Platonism can actually free us from the dialectical tensions and enable us to plumb its depths for good points and insights. Nevertheless, the central problem here is the dualistic tension of binary opposition in which all binaries require their opposites. So, pleasure requires and brings pain, death requires and brings life, and so forth. By this reasoning, time necessitates eternity, and the good requires and necessitates either evil or negation of the good. If that is true, then the eternality of the good is based on the simultaneous eternality of evil. If the two require and necessitate the others, then the value judgment of adjudicating something as "good" and something as "bad" must also be illusory and relative. And whichever appellation is chosen can logically be interchanged with the other. If both good and evil are relative terms based on the eternality of both in dualistic tension, then good is evil and evil is good, and we are back at monism. Numerous other ways of modelling this presupposition as contradictory nonsense could be given, but this should be sufficient to show that it is nonsensical on its own grounds.

In like manner, the location of knowledge of the forms is placed by Plato in past lives. Transmigration of the soul and reincarnation (clearly borrowed from older pagan religions) is nonsensical on numerous grounds, but the most obvious is the impossible bridge or link between the realm of the forms and this life of flux. How can the good, eternal, invariant, and universal actually be in our realm of the opposite? It cannot, and for Plato the only bridge between these two realms was the human intellect. Since the human intellect clearly makes connections and associations that extend beyond the empirical, how is this possible? If human autonomy and rationalistic primacy of intellect are the starting point for epistemology, then it stands to reason that the knowledge of universals we obtain must originate in past lives. However, this does not solve the problem of finitude, as the ability to link what Kant called a transcendental unity of apperception or a unitive identity in an object over time (identity over time) cannot be solved by a finite human intellect. The only way out of this dilemma is an infinite Divine Mind that contains all the *logoi* (forms) but not a human intellect. The human intellect is a small mirror of this logos, but it is not a mirror of the divine monad's essence as Platonism, Origenism, Augustinianism, and Thomism say.

Bosch's *Garden of Earthly Delights*— Forms and Archetypes

The bridge between the infinite and the finite is the human nous, a faculty given by God to know God. The human nous is able to, through remembrance of God (not remembrance of past lives), achieve actual gnosis of the logoi (forms) through union with God, not intellectual and rational accumulation of facts. The rationalist tendency to identify intellect and soul in Platonism must be rejected, as this identification is also the root of the anthropological trend the West would take, turning it to its own oblivion. The reason for this is Plato's idea that the soul, because it is invisible, must be a perfect unity like the original monad, and thus in dialectical tension, the multiplicity and flux of the body, is in tension against the perfect unity of the soul *identified with the intellect*. No, people are not dualities of body and soul in tension, but body, soul, and spirit, and by returning to God through repentance and love, their hearts (nous) are changed, thus altering their intellect by placing intellect under the rule of nous. For Plato, it was people's intellect that was primary—for orthodoxy; it was people's hearts that must change in submission to God, which cleansed the mind to submit to the nous, and thereby people perceived the truth of things (logoi). For Plato, *theosis* was achieved by people's intellect. Biblically, theosis is achieved by placing intellect under the dominance of the heart and God's law.

However, these criticisms aside, Plato's argument against naïve empiricism is excellent and crucial. In their minds, people do connect similar concepts in objects of experience, and these connecting concepts themselves are not empirically experienced. They are also not mere token terms invented by social structures, but real ideas, real connecting universals, that objects share through participation in the universal. This doctrine of participation of many things in one while retaining their identities was chosen in the patristic era because of this balance, over and against Aristotelian hylomorphism. Hylomorphism in Aristotelian thought excludes the possibility of more than one unity in an object—any singular substance must be an absolutely simple substance. However, for Plato, there was at least the notion of the balance of the one and the many in an object, which is able to share the universal characteristics of roundness, whiteness, and other characteristics without those characteristics and particularity losing their real identity, as twentieth-century British philosopher Sherrard has elucidated. Plato's arguments about forms from the problem of the one and the many are the ultimate antidote to the naïve empiricism and scientism that have so drugged the masses in our day. Socrates even jokes that, in his young days, he was taken up by the naïve empirical natural science of pre-Socratic Greek philosopher Anaxagoras (fifth century BCE) as if it was the answer to everything, only later in life coming to the realization that it was a fundamentally flawed and presuppositionally nonsensical view that attempted to explain causality by reference to other causes or descriptions. This circular, contradictory, nonsensical view was highlighted a few millennia later by eighteenth-century Scottish philosopher David Hume, who would take the skepticism of empiricism to its logical conclusions—total insanity and the destruction of all possibility of knowledge.

The Metaphysics of Creation

How are we to replace the base, contradictory narrative of humanity's "progress" with something better? Is there an answer elsewhere? Can claims of religious belief and theology be rational? Are they not merely leaps of faith with no reason behind them? In short, there are answers and religious claims just as warranted as "scientific" claims, and sometimes more so. When we consider "warranted" beliefs, as they are often termed in philosophy, we can see alternate explanations that are far superior to the reductionist materialism of our day.

It is my thesis that there is an alternate metaphysics that is suppressed by the centralized Western establishment that allows for a covert advancement in highly complex technologies while the ignorant public have been given a mass-consumption physics and worldview that is ultimately a dead end—materialism. One of the chief arguments I fall back on is that highly advanced technologies are based on a rigorous, formal logic that is ordered and perfectly systematic. Since logic itself, which forms the basis and presupposition of those systems, is not and cannot be "matter," the central narrative explanation of reality given by modern academia for humanity's origins—"enlightenment" and so-called scientific advance—is completely wrong.

This alternate metaphysics is closer to what is found in aspects of Platonism and Eastern Orthodox theology, and this is likely what informed nineteenth/twentieth-century scientist Nikola Tesla to be so successful with his inventions despite his latter-day involvement in theosophy.

I do not intend to advocate all of Platonism or Pythagoreanism or later developments in Plato's students, but rather, when considering foundational philosophical presuppositional commitments and assumptions, I will assert that the ideas of thinkers closer to this tradition are more correct than those of an atomistic, materialist bent. Modern quantum thinkers generally tend to be open about Platonic theories of metaphysics matching up to their discoveries, while materialistic science is utterly bankrupt at providing any coherent account of reality.

One of the founding fathers of quantum physics, twentieth-century German theoretical physicist Werner Heisenberg, stated:

> In the philosophy of Democritus the atoms are eternal and indestructible units of matter, they can never be transformed into each other. With regard to this question modern physics takes a definite stand against the materialism of Democritus and for Plato and the Pythagoreans. The elementary particles are certainly not eternal and indestructible units of matter, they can actually be transformed into each other. As a matter of fact, if two such particles, moving through space with a very high kinetic energy, collide, then many new elementary particles may be created from the available energy and the old particles may have disappeared in the collision. Such events have been frequently observed and offer the best proof that *all particles are made of the same substance: energy. But the resemblance of the modern views to those of Plato and the Pythagoreans can be carried somewhat further. The elementary particles in Plato's Timaeus are finally not substance but mathematical forms.*[1] (Author's italic emphasis)

"All things are numbers" is an idea attributed to Pythagoras. The only mathematical forms available at that time were such geometric forms as the regular solids or the triangles that form their surface. In modern quantum theory, there can be no doubt that the elementary particles will finally also be mathematical forms but of a much more complicated nature. The Greek philosophers thought of static forms and found them in the regular solids. Modern science, however, has, from its beginning in the sixteenth and seventeenth centuries, started from the dynamic problem. The constant element in physics since Isaac Newton in the seventeenth century is not a configuration or a geometrical form, but a dynamic law.

> The equation of motion holds at all times, it is in this sense eternal, whereas the geometrical forms, like the orbits, are changing. Therefore, the mathematical forms that represent the elementary particles will be solutions of some eternal law of motion for matter. This is a problem which has not yet been solved.[2]

The principle at work here is explained in notable philosophy of twentieth-century science writer, Michael Polanyi, who wrote:

> To say that the discovery of objective truth in science consists in the apprehension of a rationality which commands our respect and arouses our contemplative admiration, that such discovery, while using the experience of our senses as clues, transcends this experience by embracing the vision of a reality beyond the impression of our senses, a vision which speaks for itself in guiding us to an even deeper understanding of reality—such an account of scientific procedure would be generally shrugged aside as out-dated Platonism: a piece of mystery-mongering unworthy of an enlightened age. Yet it is precisely on this conception of objectivity that I wish to insist in.[3]

Ours is a day of cowardice, ignorance, and lack of real knowledge and wisdom despite the avalanche of information available at everyone's fingertips. Without a framework into which we can place information, the never-ending data stream is useless and destructive. Those who have the desire to find truth must not be afraid to go against the grain and consider options outside the so-called mainstream, not because going against the grain is somehow inherently laudatory, but because it is a time of tremendous deception. In a land of supposed free inquiry and free thought, the only thing considered untenable and anathema is Creation by a single personal god. In fact, Carl Sagan and Richard Dawkins even say we can posit alien origins, yet belief in God is somehow irrational. On the contrary, those on our side have a far superior explanation of reality that is actually coherent. A biblical worldview may not answer every single question posed, but no worldview can provide that, much less one that is fundamentally contradictory like materialism or *unobserved* eonian Darwinian evolutionary theory.

Werner Heisenberg said this about atomic orbit: "The smallest units of matter are not physical objects in the ordinary sense; they are forms, ideas which can be expressed unambiguously only in mathematical language."[4]

In response, I would like to suggest the metaphysics and philosophy of science posited by one of my favorite thinkers, Orthodox theologian and traditionalist, Dr. Philip Sherrard. Dr. Sherrard is not well known to Western academics. His concise yet brilliant approach to this question solidifies a new way to look at science based on the Eastern and biblical traditions, and it provides a unique metaphysic, the one expounded by thinkers like Saint Maximus the Confessor in the seventh century CE. I believe these ideas form a part of the hidden metaphysics I mentioned earlier. Sherrard wrote a brief but brilliant article entitled "A Single Unified Science."[5] I have included this article here, interspersed with my comments and analysis.

Sherrard writes:

> The fall may best be understood not as a moral
> deviation or as a descent into a carnal state, but
> as a drama of knowledge, as a dislocation and
> degradation of our consciousness, a lapse of our
> perceptive and cognitive powers—a lapse which
> cuts us off from the presence and awareness of other
> superior worlds and imprisons us in the fatality of
> our solitary existence in this world. It is to forget
> the symbolic function of every form and to see in
> things not their dual, symbiotic reality, but simply
> their non-spiritual dimension, their psycho-physical
> or material appearance.

Dr. Sherrard is discussing the sacred view of nature in which the
divine origin of reality is not lost in the deistic divide of God from his
direct immanent energetic presence in all reality. As I have written
elsewhere, Thomism and the Enlightenment led the West to this
great divide that formed around the theological and metaphysical
assumptions of Saint Thomas Aquinas in the thirteenth century
and then the *philosophes* of the eighteenth-century Enlightenment.
Sherrard's metaphysic matches up to the discoveries of quantum
physicists such as the notion of higher and lower dimensions.

Sherrard continues:

> Seen in this perspective, our crime, like that of
> Adam, is equivalent to losing this sense of symbols;
> for to lose the sense of symbols is to be put in the
> presence of our own darkness, of our own ignorance.
> This is the exile from Paradise, the condition of our
> fallen humanity; and it is the consequence of our
> ambition to establish our presence exclusively in
> this terrestrial world and to assert that our presence

in this world, and exclusively in this world, accords with our real nature as human beings. In fact, we have reached the point not only of thinking that the world which we perceive with our ego-consciousness is the natural world, but also of thinking that our fallen, subhuman state is the natural human state, the state that accords with our nature as human beings. And we talk of acquiring knowledge of the natural world when we do not even know what goes on in the mind of an acorn.

If the immediate perception we have is not the totality of reality, then entire worlds of possibility are opened up to us. This does not mean adopting any and every fantasy, but rather using reason, which we have from God, as a tool of revelation itself. Knowledge is very different from what modern humanity conceives it to be: It is traditional and initiatory. Contrary to common assumptions, modern humanity suffers from a fetish of the new in which the only real or true knowledge can only be ever-evolving and changing theories that are wholly overturned a year later. The futile search for a single unifying elementary particle reflects this idolatrous desire of humans to find their deity through science and not through revelation. But if knowledge is initiatic and revelatory, this quest is a dead end. Humankind's knowledge of this world is always temporal, finite, and partial, and a presuppositional commitment to a world of constant flux can give rise only to a science that is ever and always in flux with no objective certainty or purpose.

This does not mean a traditionalist approach to knowledge is never added to or refined, but rather that there is no oppositional dialectic—no old versus new, revolutionary versus archaic. There is a harmony of advance within stasis. The new can expand only on some tradition, which is why the scientific community itself is a hierarchical cultus within which knowledge is transmitted through tradition. Twenty-first-century astrophysicist Neil de Grasse Tyson has not personally experienced all the scientific experiments he has read about; he must accept them as a reliable body of doctrine based on his more fundamental worldview commitments to scientism. This is not to say Tyson is completely unwarranted in his belief in scientific journals; rather, it is to say that he, like a religious believer, has unexamined, non-empirical faith commitments that inform his modus operandi in the world.

Sherrard continues:

> This dislocation of our consciousness which defines the fall is perhaps most clearly evident in the divorce we make between the spiritual and the material, the esoteric and the exoteric, the uncreated and the created, and in our assumption that we can know the one without knowing the other. If we acknowledge the spiritual realm at all, we tend to regard it as something quite other than the material realm and to deny that the Divine is inalienably present in natural forms or can be known except through a direct perception which bypasses the natural world— as though the existence of this world were, spiritually speaking, negative and of no consequence where our salvation is concerned.[6]

This other-worldly type of esotericism only too often degenerates into a kind of spiritual debauchery, in the sense that it has its counterpart in the idea that it is possible to cultivate the inner spiritual life, and to engage in meditation, invocation, and other ritual practices, whether consecrated or counterfeit, while our outward life, professional or private, is lived in obedience to mental and physical standards and habits that not only have nothing spiritual about them but are completely out of harmony with the essential rhythms of being: Divine, human, and natural. We should never forget that an authentic spiritual life can be lived only on condition, first, that the way in which we represent to ourselves the physical universe, as well as our own place in it, accords with the harmony instilled into its whole structure through the Divine which brings it into, and sustains it in, existence; and second, that insofar as is humanly possible, we conform every aspect of our life—mental, emotional, and physical—to this harmony, disengaging therefore from all activity and practice which patently clash with it. If we offend against the essential rhythms of being, then our aspirations to tap the wellspring of our spiritual life are condemned to fruitlessness, or in some cases may even lead to a state of psychic disequilibrium that can, in truth, be described as demonic.

This is a hard pill for modern thinkers to swallow or even consider. If modern physicalism and naturalistic explanations are not correct, people may have erred in their ideological trek out of "self-imposed slavery" into Enlightenment scientism. The stages of nineteenth-century philosopher Auguste Comte's advancement may actually be backwards. Comte's positivistic and rationalistic theory of history posited that humans progressed from religion to metaphysics and philosophy and then to science. In fact, the inverse may be the case—people find that their science needs a unifying principle and foundation that is not provided by impersonalistic philosophies and rationalist speculations. Instead, true knowledge of the world may be had more readily in a tradition that provides a framework for things science uses like math and logic. In fact, modern atheism and materialism are more like something demonic than mere ideology, which explains why more people have died in world wars and under secular, atheistic, materialistic regimes in the twentieth century than in all previous religious conflicts combined.

Sherrard continues:

> The divorce between the spiritual and the material means that material forms are regarded as totally non-spiritual, and thus either as illusion or as only to be known through identifying their reality with their purely material aspects. Such a debasement of the physical dimension of things is tantamount not only to denying the spiritual reality of our own created existence, but also, through depriving natural things of their theophanic function, to treating a Divine revelation as a dead and soulless body. And in this case it is not only of a kind of suicide that we are speaking; we are also speaking of a kind of murder.
>
> It is just as dangerous to think we can attain knowledge of God while ignoring, or even denying, His presence in existing things and in their corresponding symbolic rituals as it is for us to think that we can attain knowledge of existing things while ignoring, or even denying, the Divine presence that informs them and gives them their reality. In effect, there cannot be knowledge of the outward appearance of things—of what we call phenomena—without knowledge of their inner reality; just as there cannot be knowledge of this inner reality which does not include a knowledge of the outer appearance.

Sherrard hits on a crucial insight into the metaphysics of unbelief, if you will. These always devolve into monism or solipsism where external reality is illusory, or the internal reality of mind or soul is illusory. Materialism, by its definition, can never escape the strange loop of cyclical nonsense and incoherence and must give way to ultimate irrationality and holistic negation. Unless the world is seen as a theophanic revelation of the Divine Mind and the logoi, there is no unifying principle for Creation. All that is left to unify reality is the finite mind of humanity, which is only a mirror of an unknown external existence of phantasms and flux, never attaining any capability beyond linguistic constructs about knowing external reality.

Sherrard concludes:

> It is the same as with the Holy Book: the integrality of the revelation cannot be understood simply from its letter, from its outward literal sense; it can be understood only when interpreted by the spiritual science of its inner meaning. At the same time this inner meaning cannot be perceived except by means of the letter, of the outward literal sense. There is an unbreakable union between the esoteric and the exoteric, the feminine and the masculine, between the inner reality of a thing and its external appearance. And any genuine knowledge of either depends upon both being regarded as integers of a single unified science.

Just as a tradition and contextual worldview of nature is required before it can be "interpreted," so does any book, including the Bible. There is no purely neutral footing on which a person, as a blank slate, can create a fresh, new meaning for the world or a book; people are always bound by the inherited lexicon from which they have emerged. This is not to say all beliefs are culturally relative; rather, a cultural and semantic lexicon of some kind is something passed on to all, and this fact is inescapable. People all learn the particular

Jay Dyer

language of the culture into which they are born. They learn in some academic institution and are informed (or misinformed) by other institutions, like religion.

Without a tradition and a worldview to inform science, science is not a search for knowledge or truth, but a tool of power politics enforced by the nastiest oligarchs to benefit their own goals. Science becomes scientism, the baseless ideology of a technocratic state with no other telos than the perpetuation of the technocratic corporate state itself. Might now makes right because there is no truth; truth is simply established by the entity with the most "stuff," whether material or virtual. The removal of telos from the world, and thus from the divine from the world, is the replacement with the great monadic particle god of flux, and his cultus, the fetish of the ever-new. Yet the ever-new that must constantly be churned out constantly denies eternal truth and permanence and so negates itself nihilistically as irrelevant. Religion then degenerates according to this destructive scientistic spirit, becoming a mirror of the consumerist plastic society in which it dwells. Without a metaphysical basis, science is meaningless. If ultimate reality is irrational, humankind's finitely constructed subjective meaning is a drop in a vast ocean of universal meaninglessness. Modern humans and their scientism are ultimately doomed to nihilism as the empty promises of scientific progress tell people their lives are pointless, and with it all of their science.

Notes:

1
2   Werner Heisenberg, _Physics and Philosophy: The Revolution in Modern Science_ (New York: Harper Perennial Modern Classics, 1958).
3   (_Personal Knowledge_, p. 5–6)
4
5
6

CHAPTER 3

The Philosophy of Creation

One of the most difficult things for moderns to apprehend is the seemingly counter-intuitive worldview of modified Platonism. This reorientation shifts our entire perspective on the outer, external world, rendering it again a sacred space infused with the divine, as opposed to a brute "material" realm dominated by chaos, entropy, and death. Our contemporaries nonetheless prefer the latter grand narrative (and a depressing narrative it is) that proclaims that we in the other camp are "weak" for choosing older "fictions" like souls, angels, and God. To be sure, the materialists and servants of delusion of brute matter have their own deity—the impersonal forces of nature—but we'll set that aside for the moment.

It is crucial that the psyche must undergo this repentance—*metanoia* in Greek—and reorienting, as the modern attitude is that of fallen humanity, who view their world as devoid of supernatural under the guise of "science." While the scientific method is certainly a useful tool, the lack of philosophical education on the part of that community is appalling. Precisely the hubris of fallen humans impels the hierophants of the naturalist cult to stamp out all such ideas— even the slightest tendency toward the idea that the psyche or mind may not be reduced to chemical reactions must be swiftly punished.

This is why the discoveries and theses proposed in quantum physics are so disturbing to advocates of scientism despite their good faith in future science to resolve all questions of being with strict rationalism. Never mind the fact that "reason" itself is nonsensical in the deterministic paradigm of Darwinian naturalism; the crusaders of modern empiricism are committed adherents of the holy inquisition of scientism, and no manner of logical argumentation can persuade them otherwise. Those aware of an alternate version of human history, the biblical narrative, in which humans are fallen creatures in rebellion against their Creator, have a perfectly rational (indeed, the only rational) explanation of these events, and can even explain why people prefer their own self-imposed servitude, quoting Kant, rather than submission to the doctrine of Creation.

Creation is essential because of the implications it conveys for the entirety of how people perceive the world and operate in it. Our worldview determines the way we act, showing the old adage of *lex orandi, lex credendi* to be correct. If the universe is a created reality, then the implications for how things like electrons, matter, and other natural entities work have vastly different meanings. For example, if there is no Creation, and the universe is either eternal or illusory, the way we operate will be dictated accordingly. We can look to history to show us civilizations in which such a fundamental presupposition dominated, such as Hindu India or ancient China. In these cultures, the dominance of the absolute as an impersonal reality, with a multitude of lesser deities to be supplicated, created a vast array of self-destructive practices amongst the populations. Starvation reigned in India while cattle roamed free as divine, and a "divine" emperor held sway in China where individual subjects had no personal identity. These are merely examples of basic philosophical presuppositions that undergirded a culture and resulted in a praxis consistent therewith.

Precisely because these civilizations were suffused with the notion that time and the universe were eternal, existence itself became a trap. The wheel of time and materiality had to be escaped through meditation, radical asceticism, or some other form of mystical gnosis. If, on the other hand, "material" reality was a created reality and not a self-subsisting eternal principle of its own, and the fundamental framework of the "stuff" of reality was designed and had begun at a point in time, the implications would be vastly different. The Creation account in Genesis, for example, presents a very different narrative of history and its beginnings than these other accounts. Although it has been fashionable for the last few hundred years to dismiss the Genesis narrative as a fictional mythology of numerous blended ancient Near Eastern cosmologies, the fact remains that the Creation account in Genesis presents a vastly different theology than is presented in any other religious Creation story aside from the Egyptian.

This difference cannot be overstated: the biblical account posits that time and "matter" are not evils, traps, or the source of any fundamentally oppositional principle, but are rather good— inherently good, due to being created *in time by a good God*. God, being good, does not "create" evil as if it had any substantial or ontological being. All being, in the metaphysical sense and the here and now, is created being, and created with the potential to receive the higher divine energies or powers of God. Creation was placed in a state in which it might be raised to even higher good, though I'm not implying that Creation was therefore bad because its initial state was a lesser good. There is no opposition or dialectic between the good being many, as later Western philosophy, Platonism in particular, would posit. This opposition of the good necessarily being absolutely one (the simple monad), was a Platonic idea that would have its precedent in ancient Far Eastern thought.

Even the Hellenistic hermetic texts and the Egyptian accounts in the Memphite narrative, for example, include the idea that Creation was spoken into existence by virtue of a divine logos, yet the overall principle, the ultimate absolute, is not personal, but an immaterial force. At the outset, we are presented with only two possible options for this question—is the absolute (supra) rational and personal, or is the absolute an impersonal, chaotic force? There are only two possibilities here, and once we consider this basic philosophical question, we can extrapolate Darwinism as a clear manifestation of the second. Though most Darwinian adherents would be at pains to insist there is no ultimate guiding principle, their worldview still tends toward the notion of forces of nature determining existence. This determination, however, is ultimately irrational and impersonal, aside from the appearance of order, telos, and design. (Note that I am not making a classical teleological argument, but a transcendental version of a teleological argument.)

But there are many more problems for positing ultimate reality or the absolute as an impersonal force. If ultimate reality is impersonal and chaotic, then all localized events, phenomena, and objects are also devoid of any ultimate meaning. Language, mathematics, logic, and other disciplines are thus annihilated as merely mental fictions, or at best some cosmic force we do not yet understand.

The high priests of Darwinism, servants of chaos and the abyss, resemble the proverbial cartoon character who saws off the limb he sits upon to spite his opponent. If ultimate reality is impersonal, then the teleological thread that links all facts, ideas, objects, patterns, and so forth is not real. It is a fiction of humanity's chaotic, impersonal mental chemical reactions. There is no order or pattern actually out there in external reality, and the so-called regularity of nature upon which science is built—induction—is merely a mental projection or interpretation. Such devastating eventualities, of course, are the very reason science (or scientism) has chosen to discard philosophy as useless. However, these matters cannot be evaded, and science never determines reality by some will-to-power dismissal of philosophical questions. The mere fact that "scientists" dogmatically mandate that *no one can ask questions about why or what happened before the so-called big bang* demonstrates only how futile and absurd their posturing is.

Creation becomes the only logical and philosophically coherent position to explain existence as it renders the very principle of coherence itself sensible as an objective reality. Despite the insistence of the Darwinian and scientistic rationalists that they alone hold the keys of reason, they have dug a pit they themselves have fallen into, to cite Psalm 7:15. Reason, coherence, pattern recognition, mathematics, and logic are not mental constructs, but undeniably operative principles in the objective, external world. This is how bridges are built, how words facilitate communication, and how the principle of induction makes science possible. This is also how geometry is math in space and how music is math in time. Precisely because these principles work in the world to build amazing logic machines, like computers, we can see how the basic presuppositions of the reductionist-naturalist are false.

Here we continually return to the question of objective metaphysical principles as the means by which to engage the opponent and modernity as a whole. Our disagreement begins with Creation and what the world is. It is guided by an omniscient, omnipotent, omnipresent God, and all the stuff of reality has its ground in a single Divine Mind. Reality is, at base, rational, although that rationality is infinite, and so it transcends our finite reason. Regardless, it does not make God irrational; it makes Him supra-rational, which means there are plenty of things we must learn analogically. In contrast, for the opponents, reality is ultimately irrational with no meaning, telos, or guiding principle. It just is, and that brute nihilism is something opponents must continually confront as they seek to make reason, science, and math function as a supposed mental fiction in the external world.

For the unhappy materialist, the world is not something to be ruled as a steward under a good God; rather, it is a dark, chaotic, nihilistic, empty place upon which meaning must be imposed, not discovered. This is precisely why scientism has so often succumbed to brutality and the rape of nature despite its never-ending claim to worship nature and exalt environmentalism. It is the impetus of social Darwinism to ultimately seek the destruction of nature, as nature is not a sacred manifestation of the Divine Mind and beauty, but a merely harsh ruler to overthrow, annihilate, and "perfect" (through transhumanism and the synthetic rewrite). However, if we in theology are correct, this grand plan is doomed to fail because people are not gods who determine meaning and objective reality. People are stewards of God made with the plan to be made divine and immortal in God's way, and not in fallen humanity's rebellious way.

Recent discoveries in quantum physics validate the traditional worldview, moreover, as its theses consider the fundamental substrate of reality to be information. We see this in DNA research and in quantum perspectives of subatomic reality. Discoveries of the holographic model of reality are merely confirmations of the platonic models of psyche and idea as the fundamental substrate of reality. We are witnessing a revolution that runs completely contrary to the empirical British Royal Society narrative we have so long been fed, truly heralding the fall of the old Enlightenment empiricism. To poison the well and control the narrative, however, New Agers and the think tanks have jumped on board, and already we have brigades of baloney salesmen attempting to hijack quantum physics for whatever scam the establishment rolls out.

We remind readers that critiques made of absolute impersonalism equally apply to the New Age syncretists' hijacking of quantum physics. The fact that the fundamental substrate of humans and "matter" is information, and more specifically energetic information, speaks to a worldview necessitating an infinite, omniscient mind to order all of reality. Without an infinite mind linking all the particulars, the connections we make are illusory. For metaphysics and philosophy and science to work, we need a rational, linking principle. We need something to hold all this substrate, all these patterns, all these principles together—and the finite human mind is never enough.

Ancient tradition in Genesis, a Creation narrative, explains reality as the Creation of a loving God, and as a reflection of eternal principles and archetypes in His mind—called logoi—that are all one in His logos, or Word. In the first chapter of Genesis, the universe is spoken into existence through divine fiat and contains within it a fundamental meaning. That fundamental informational meaning, exemplified in something like DNA, is grounded in the eternal, whence its purpose derives. Humanity, as creatures of God, can thus make advances and learn about the world—even though both humanity and the world are fallen—as they progress back toward union with God and the eventual renewal of all things in God. Only in this paradigm with these presuppositions are science, reason, meaning, logic, and mathematics even possible and coherent. Our own minds are little mirrors of the one Divine Mind, each a microcosmos to contemplate the many.

CHAPTER 4

The Problem of Scientism

Ours is the great transition age. For the masses, the glowing assumption is that the revolutionary period we are undergoing is the work of a long evolutionary process of natural progress. Wandering about their bubbles, the hipster proletarians neither challenge nor examine these presuppositions, rather decorating their cafeteria-plate lives with long strings of media-generated buzzwords and empty slogans overheard in establishment schooling. "We are evolving," "We live in an era of change," and numerous other advertising blurbs that underlie modernity's plastic ideology actually form the basis for most of humanity's worldview. Yet are any of these assumptions actually true? Are we in living in an era of progress and human ascent?

I'll answer in the negative, and the reasons for a dark assessment are many. Listening recently to someone of a truly skeptical bent interview a figure in the scientism/skeptical crowd, I was irked to hear a bevy of fallacies, incongruencies, and unexamined assumptions that I will analyze here with scalpel-like precision. As I have mentioned, what precisely is meant by the terms *evolution, change, progress,* and *nature*? According to those in the ranks of establishment scientism, these are givens, terms of brute factuality and reason, all of which mystically coalesce to give us the best possible model of the world under the new grand narrative mythos of science.

What is meant by evolution? According to modern scientism, the observation of small-scale changes in a species that appear to aid in the extension of the species into the future through reproduction is the basic understanding of evolutionary adaptation. Thus, because certain breeds of animals can be bred with fitter members of the species, we can extrapolate that large-scale eons of time resulted in the origins of all life from a single amoeba. When it is pointed out that eons—millions of years—of adaptation and change are not observed, the reply is that bacteria purportedly adapt under conditions of pressure. Thus, it follows that all life mutated under conditions of pressure to "evolve" into what we see today.

On the surface, this carries the appearance of being reasonable. Almost no one denies micro-evolutionary adaptation and change and that, within the mechanics of various organisms, there resides the DNA programming to adapt to environmental circumstances. The bait and switch comes with the dogmatic assertion that, from this observation, it is certain that all life originated from a single cell millions of years ago, following billions of years of big bang expansion. The evidence for such theories nowadays is, of course, taken as dogmatic fact with any dissension on these matters scorned and mocked. Why? Because religion is irrational and unscientific and cannot be tested. Yet can these assertions be tested as scientific?

The standard reply is that they are proven by carbon dating and observing various UV rays that appear to "expand" from the presumed "singularity" point. There are numerous problems with these claims, but the most glaring will suffice as an illustration. First, carbon dating is notoriously unreliable; examples of testing on recent artifacts showing outrageous time stamps for items that are manifestly not ancient. Further, carbon dating itself works on the assumption of millions of years of evolutionary chaotic flux, which begs questioning. In other words, if your testing methods already operate on the assumption that matter is eons in age, then the results of the tests are obviously predetermined.

Second, the appearance of light expanding from some locale is only as coherent as the assumption that it comes from some point of singularity, and there is absolutely no observable evidence of this. When these facts are pointed out to those enmeshed in the religion of scientism, many respond that these practices and beliefs are "theories" but they are "the best models we have." Says who exactly? Why will the adherents to scientism never admit they are subject to biases and greed (for the winning of grants)? How is it that science lab is magically averse to the failings of the rest of human endeavors? "Ah, well, yes," the general response comes. "It is subject to those things, but that is the beauty of science. We are always changing and adapting our theories to fit the evidence."

To a degree, this is true. Science does posit new theories and does refine its previous analyses as new data emerges. Yet, as I've pointed out many times, for this methodology to be consistent, scientific experiments into the question of the empirical scientific method itself, as well as its governing assumptions, would also have to be conducted. This is never, ever done aside from one establishment-funded study that tried to implicate lab bias into a ridiculous Marxist framework. On the contrary, there is a motivating impetus to *not* conduct this kind of investigation because it would expose much of scientism's fraud and deception. It would disclose that the scientific establishment is the servant of the same master as the banking, economic, and entertainment establishments, all of which operate under the (fallacious) umbrella of consensus reality.

The scientific establishment is a hierarchy that operates just like any other corporation or government entity in which knowledge is apportioned on a need-to-know basis. Biologists are afraid, for example, to speak on the matter of physics because they aren't physicists, while mathematicians are afraid to speak on the matter of astronomy because they aren't astronomers. This ridiculous segmentation of knowledge (and there is nothing wrong with specialization) is also predicated on the presupposition of scientism that reality is not a meaningful, coherent universe, but a random, chaotic mutation of accidental consequence. "It just is" becomes the scientistic refrain, and if you don't accept that premise and consider any other options, you *must be* a fool.

What begins to become clear is that this is a weighted game that has nothing to do with discovering what is true, objective, and "factual" in the "natural world," but rather, those in the position of gatekeepers demand adherence to a predefined set of orthodoxies that determines who is a "scientist" and who is worthy of "peer review." Furthermore, scientism is entirely grounded in an old, outdated epistemology known as empiricism, which has been dissected, refuted, and annihilated so many times by cogent philosophers and logicians that its continued existence is ironically miraculous. Of all the persons who ought to adhere to their much-touted logic and reason, these fools are the most irrational, incoherent, and nonsensical of all, as they perpetually melt under the hundred-degree flame of foundational presuppositional inquiry. (And that's a lab test I've done many times that appears to always hold true.)

Arrogantly assuming they know, when in fact they do not (instead they adopt a gadfly's appearance of knowledge), adherents of scientism fancy logic only when it suits them, quickly discarding and dispensing with such rigors when the heat comes. The idea that all human knowledge comes through sensory experience sets their assumptions, yet when pressed as to whether this proposition itself is a fact of sensory data (which it obviously is not), universal claims suddenly dissipate, and this great commandment is hailed as an obvious given. It's a new maxim, a new commandment from the gods of the Enlightenment, and we dare not ask such questions. Yet, if science is so groundbreaking and revolutionary in character, why are its high priests so afraid of these basic questions of epistemology?

The general refrain at this stage is that science cannot, should not, and will not answer such absurd metaphysical questions. Now wait a minute here—on what basis did this suddenly get shelved into the metaphysical category? What standards separate metaphysical data from lab data? One begins to see how many and multifaceted the mere assumptions are for scientism to operate. Despite the fact that their starting point is a foundational contradiction, the rest of the world is expected to gaze in awe upon all the edifices that are constructed upon these fallacies with rational inquiry unwelcomed. This, you see, is the role of philosophy, and that's quite clearly the reason true philosophical inquiry is hated by the votaries of scientism (as Tyson recently demonstrated).

Also crucial to note is the structure of scientism and the establishment. Their fraudulent bases are continuously exposed openly, and the public is none the wiser. This year alone papers were produced as a result of peer review that suggest that black holes are both impossible and nonexistent. Other papers insisted they exist. "Dark matter" pervades our universe; yet, wait … no, it's back to ancient conceptions of ether. Quantum physics is real, yet, wait … it is pseudo-science theory. In other words, science, like all the other industries, operates under the public's naïve assumption that it is a unified, governing body of nonbiased, neutral geniuses who are engaged in the noble endeavor of furthering the progress of human knowledge. Again we see those amorphous, undefined, inchoate terms.

Simple philosophical questions should come to bear on these multitudes of theories, and were scientists better trained in logic and metaphysics (they are not), we might avoid many of these ridiculous pitfalls. For example, if Einstein's relativity is true, there is no fixed point of reference from which to determine which stellar bodies are orbiting which. Neither could we prove the theory that the universe expanded from a single, compressed atomic mass. This preposterous notion is a clear signpost of the irrationality of scientism, as is the popular theory of how planets formed—that random chunks of space dust (like belly button lint) got caught in orbits, started spinning, and over billions of years congealed into a sphere from which life happened to spring forth from primal sludge. Truly it is the case that only academics could believe such fairy tales that are far more laughable than religious Creation narratives.

And so, the age of transition is not the transition into the era of utopian scientific progress, transhumanism, technological immortality, and United Nations kumbaya togetherness most imagine; it is the age of transitioning away from all traditional forms of culture. It is the age of transition into a new global mythology that is created and manufactured in the same way the culture industry creates cultures in various societies under its control. It is a scientific dictatorship that is not scientific, but dogmatic, fascistic, and hierarchically structured on a need-to-know basis that blatantly hides, obfuscates, and rejects actual data and information about human origins and life, only to replace it with the most preposterous theories of primal sludge, lint ball planets, and imagined eons of unobserved billions of years meaninglessly exploding forth from the universe's (Fantasia-level) singularity point.

This is not progress; such imbecilic theories are a regression into explanatory models with no explanatory power. They need to be called out for what they are—replacement mythologies that are rehashed forms of ancient atomism dressed up in scientistic garb. It is time to reject these phonies, liars, dupes, and establishment hacks, and recognize how they suppress real science and inquiry for the purpose of control. Their control is not about human progress, but the Orwellian opposite—it is a dysgenics program to destroy humanity. We need only think of *The Lancet*, Oxford's most prestigious medical journal, whose editor recently stated in a matter-of-fact tone that half the world's scientific literature is fraudulent. Dr. Horton recently published a statement declaring that a lot of published research is in fact unreliable at best, if not completely false:

> The case against science is straightforward: much
> of the scientific literature, perhaps half, may simply
> be untrue. Afflicted by studies with small sample
> sizes, tiny effects, invalid exploratory analyses,
> and flagrant conflicts of interest, together with an
> obsession for pursuing fashionable trends of dubious
> importance, science has taken a turn toward
> darkness.[1]

This turn toward darkness is quite disturbing given the fact that all of these studies (which are industry sponsored) are used to develop drugs and vaccines to supposedly help people, train medical staff, educate medical students, and drive the medical "industry" forward.

It's common for many people to dismiss valuable work by experts and researchers at various institutions around the globe which isn't peer reviewed and doesn't appear in credible medical journals, but as we can see, peer reviewed doesn't really mean much anymore. Medical journals that were once considered credible continue to lose their tenability in the eyes of experts and employees of the journals themselves, like Dr. Horton.

The Lancet's editor also went on to call himself out in a sense, stating that journal editors aid and abet the worst behaviors, that the amount of bad research is alarming, and that data is sculpted to fit a preferred theory. He observed that important confirmations are often rejected and little is done to correct bad practices. What's worse, much of what goes on could even be considered borderline misconduct.

Dr. Marcia Angell, a physician and longtime editor in chief of the *New England Journal of Medicine* (NEJM), which is considered to be another one of the most prestigious peer-reviewed medical journals in the world, makes her view of the subject quite plain:

> It is simply no longer possible to believe much of the clinical research that is published, or to rely on the judgment of trusted physicians or authoritative medical guidelines. I take no pleasure in this conclusion, which I reached slowly and reluctantly over my two decades as an editor of the *New England Journal of Medicine*.[2]

Notes:

1
2

● CHAPTER 5 ●

Paradigm Models and Loops

We often hear from those dominated by the notion of science (so called) that models of reality can never be grand narratives again, just as the fact that the conceptual framework used to explain the world cannot be extrapolated onto the external world with certainty due to the "fact" that the explanatory models themselves are purely human conceptual frameworks. Explanatory models are not true, we are told, because they have explanatory power. Thus, Newtonian physics is no longer accurate because it breaks down at the subatomic level. From Kant in the eighteenth century onward, the West has adopted the mistaken notion that no mental framework can accurately and with firm certainty be predicated of external reality. This perceived wisdom dominates academia, particularly in scientific circles. Epistemology is a no-man's-land because Kant purportedly demonstrated that empirical knowledge can never penetrate the noumenal realm.

But is this true? This is all poppycock and hogwash, and every argument the so-called scientific establishment uses to foist this upon impressionable young college minds is utterly flawed bullshit. In fact, the claim that all conceptual models are only models is itself a foundational conceptual claim that purports to position its arrogant pontificator in a place of high epistemic privilege. "We just don't know," it spews forth, "whether the concepts in our minds match up to the actual facts of the external world." However, if we follow this flawed train, it also follows that we don't know that our claims of a lack of knowledge are accurate. In other words, to say all models of reality are flawed because they cannot demonstrate that they obtain for the objects of perception is equally applicable to the universal claim that all models of reality are flawed and cannot certainly obtain for the external world. In fact, the purveyor of this bad argument is generally unaware of basics of linguistic philosophy.

Linguistic philosophy, in fact, points directly back to the reemergence of metaphysics. But metaphysics is what modernity doesn't want to talk about because of the still-dominant Enlightenment phantom empiricism. Though Enlightenment empiricism has been refuted a thousand times over, like bin Laden appearing out of hiding, it magically seems to emerge from the philosophical grave to wreak intellectual havoc. And now, a whole crop of "new atheists" who harp all day about the outdated classical arguments for theism furiously slap away at keyboards resurrecting the outdated arguments for classical empiricism and materialism. So much for intellectual honesty. One simple way to refute this fallacy with linguistic philosophy is to show that the very symbols used by the so-called skeptic of models—and by the use of language itself— require a complex set of metaphysical preconditions that must obtain for the very possibility of language at all. I have written about this before, but it functions well here as a refutation of this common error. Consider this claim: All models of reality are purely human-devised mental constructs that help us explain reality.

Every letter in this sentence is a symbol that stands for reality. Each grouping of symbols on a higher level stands for a more specific concept. *A* combines with *L* and another *L* to have a definite meaning. Meaning itself becomes a focal point of metaphysical difficulties that any empiricist must avoid like the plague. Yet the desire to avoid metaphysics because it is tough for your own faulty model is not how truth is obtained. When the three letters are combined, the concept of all models becomes clear, and when all the symbols are combined, we have a universal statement about a given state of affairs in the world. Even if this statement is to deny that we know about given sets of affairs in the world, it is still, at a base level, a factual claim about states of affairs that have obtained. On another level, it also makes a sweeping claim for a universal state of affairs.

It purports to say that *all* human models are flawed. If all human models are flawed then we can have no linguistic philosophical basis for statements about statements themselves because a self-referential statement about statements is still a statement about a given state of affairs. In essence, this claim attempts to have a privileged position from which to sound humble, claiming that models of reality are only mental realities that cannot be shown to correlate to reality. Yet the action of making this statement, even if turned in on itself and analyzed as self-referential amounts to this thought: All statements about models of reality are humanly devised construct models about models.

This is nonsense from the perspective of the enlightenment rationalist who would be forced to espouse it, but it does illustrate that there is a strange loop that occurs in these kinds of phenomena, as Douglas Hoffstadter wrote about in his book *Gödel, Escher, Bach: an Eternal Golden Braid*. Kurt Gödel showed, in set theory, that any statement about a set can be made only within set theories. We cannot find a set theory basis for set theory. It loops back upon itself—a strange loop. But strange loops are not only true of mathematics and useful for refuting the Bertrand Russells of the world who tell us that reality is reductionistic (that we can encompass everything in mathematics or materialism). On the contrary, what Gödel said about sets is well known to those who have studied presuppositional apologetics or who have read about worldviews or who understand Husserl's phenomenology. In fact, it is precisely those materialistic "sciency" Russell types who so dogmatically tout logic and mathematical reasoning.

And now you've had your ass handed to you because the logic of logic is a strange loop. The logic of logic demonstrates that, in this dimension, you do not have a privileged position from which things of this nature are not self-referential. The math of math shows that numbers do correspond to reality. They are not purely human mental entities or constructs. The logic of math that Husserl sought is precisely the fact that essences will, and must, return as Pauli said. Meaning demands telos—purpose. And that purpose demands more than a finite mind constructing all its eventualities. But it is this fact that points everything literally to an Omniscient Mind—to God. And that is what people do not want to see, and they will be stuck in the wheel of the loop of this world until they do.

CHAPTER 6

Desolation and Redemption

In *The Sickness unto Death: A Christian Psychological Exposition for Upbuilding and Awakening*, Søren Kierkegaard, nineteenth-century Danish philosopher and theologian, worked within the scope of an Augustinian tripartite view of humanity, arguing that our existential dilemma is one of despair. Augustine was relevant since he also underwent his own existential crisis in the famed *tolle lege* incident in which his world of licentious pleasures came tumbling down as he realized the finitude and emptiness of his own being. Ever since, the West has been in a dialectical battle with itself as philosophy works out this same tension present within each person.

As a person confronts himself or herself, as Kierkegaard said, the essential self is the transcendence of the self as related to itself. This self is spirit, and it's important to notice the correction Kierkegaard though he was rendering to Hegel, eighteenth/nineteenth-century German philosopher. For Hegel, the universal was the real, and the ideal alone was real. Where Kant erected a boundary between the individual mind and the noumenal realm, Hegel sought to tear down that divide by making the ideal and the ideal alone, real. This rationalist project was rejected by Kierkegaard and turned on its head.

The actual universal confronted by humanity is death, and our confrontation with death demonstrates to us as individuals our own finitude. Finitude and the infinite eternality of death or the next life is thus a dialectical struggle for us. In *The Sickness unto Death*, Kierkegaard described the self is spirit. This appears to be modelled after the Augustinian conception of the trinitarian analogue of humanity's being, which was based on the relational definition of the divine persons. In that Augustinian and Thomistic scheme, person *was* relation, but for Kierkegaard, the true self was that which transcended the dialectic of self in relation to itself, which was held captive by the determination of despair occasioned by an outside force being allowed to determine the self.

This clearly laid the groundwork for twentieth-century French existentialist Jean-Paul Sartre's distinction between being *in* itself and being *for* itself, in which the individual is condemned to be free and must not hide behind various collectivist masks and facade identities that are exteriorly determined. Despair is the means by which we reach this conversion, if you will. Part of the difficulty here is the desire for people to escape from a philosophy in which they are determined, and their own beings are conceived of as inherently evil. This notion derives from third-century Manichaeanism and characterizes the belief system of the younger Augustine prior to his conversion to Catholicism.

Manichaeanism posits dualism: an inherently evil physical existence as well as an ideal, disembodied good existence—the kingdom of light that is thought. Here, there is a matter-spirit dualism that is retained in Martin Luther's own psychological issues and determinism, but also in the rest of Western humanity's angst. The determinism versus free will debate comes into dialectical opposition as much as does the spirit versus matter and self versus other dualities. The Hegelian approach was to seek a rationalist synthesis in which the Universal Mind worked itself out in a grand historical process, while Kierkegaard rejected this as rationalist folly. From a theological perspective, it is interesting to note that these are many of the same issues raised to the fore by Eastern Orthodox critics of the Western tradition, as made evident in Dr. Joseph Farrell's *God, History and Dialectic.*

For Luther, as it was for many of these thinkers, humans are determined creatures, entirely determined by divine predestination, as Luther argued at length in *On the Bondage of the Will,* published in 1525 in response to the ides of Desiderius Erasmus, Dutch philosopher and Catholic theologian. What retains the primacy in Luther, as it eventually emerged in his master Augustine, is the primacy of volition over reason. For Augustine, the heart was what mattered in the long run, and this prepared the way for Luther's introspective mental act of *sola fide* (justification by faith). This is the milieu in which Kierkegaard, a Danish Lutheran, proposed the idea of self-transcending self-versus-itself duality, and freedom as an action against an Augustinian and Lutheran determinism as well as rejecting the spirit-matter dualism.

What is retained, however, is the self-reaching self-consciousness by the act of willing itself and not by being determined. However, what this all demonstrates is the absurd frustration that Western people created for themselves by adopting a bizarre philosophy in which dialectics are sought to be overcome by adopting a philosophy of Christianity, in which God becomes man, and man becomes God, and the meaning of happiness and blessedness is despair and misery. No wonder Kierkegaard despaired, and no wonder Friedrich Nietzsche would reject this religion in the nineteenth century.

In the course of what is now known as continental philosophy, three figures stand out as preeminent thinkers who were able to probe the innermost depths of the human psyche in a way previously unknown since perhaps Shakespeare: Søren Kierkegaard, Friedrich Nietzsche, and Fyodor Dostoevsky. These great thinkers were more or less contemporaries in the nineteenth century, and all shared a similar fascinating interest—that of tearing down the ideological idols of their day, and in particular, the facade the individual post-Enlightenment "modern" people conceived themselves to be. While these men certainly had differing worldviews and would likely have debated such grand topics as the precise meaning of God and our relation to Him in the universe, they shared a similar distaste for hypocrisy, inaccuracies, and falsehoods, and they made it partly their authorial iconoclastic goal to tear away such veils.

Sixteenth/seventeenth-century English philosopher and statesman Francis Bacon made it his goal as an early Enlightenment luminary to tear down what he perceived to be idols in his *Novum Organum*—idols of the tribe, cave, marketplace, and theater. Idols of the tribe meant the destruction of abstracted social ideals foisted upon reality: idols of the cave referred to myopic interpretations of reality according to a particular fancy of some individual academic; idols of the marketplace referred to the misappropriation of word and thing, assigning an undue identification between the two, assuming that out talking an opponent has then caused the reality of the topic under discussion to actually exist as such; and idols of the theater referred to ideas that were erected on false presuppositions of theology or metaphysical speculation and become ensconced in the public discourse.[1] This tractate encompasses the impetus of the Enlightenment and its obsession with what twentieth-century French intellectual René Guénon called the "reign of quantity." Everything is measured and classified according to some quantitative stricture of people's reason. Scientific knowledge, or more specifically, scientism, becomes the dominant paradigm by which all things are measured, be it religion, politics, economics, or the marketplace. All things are *in potentia* capable of rational formalization and, like a big algorithm, all of humanity's ills simply await the solution of the academy and its laboratory calculators.

Kierkegaard, Nietzsche, and Dostoevsky would take this same methodology and turn it in on itself. Is it possible that Bacon and his Enlightenment progeny were guilty of the very things he sought to destroy? Did the *philosophes* erect idols of their own? The influence of Kierkegaard on Nietzsche must first be mentioned. Kierkegaard struggled with the complacency and formalism of the Lutheran official church of his day, resulting in an introspective journey that caused him to question even the nature of the self. Kierkegaard did not, however, analyze the self from some kind of privileged, abstracted "scientific" view as did others like Descartes and his cogito; rather, he explored the dialectical relationship of the self with itself and the other. In *The Sickness unto Death*, he concluded that the self must come to despair (the sickness) and, reveling in its own finitude, find solace in a relationship with an infinite God. For Kierkegaard, this was the only way to escape the continual dialectic fallen human, trapped by virtue of being a son of Adam.

Twenty/twenty-first-century professor and critic Merold Westphal wrote:

> For these three secular masters of suspicion [Marx, Nietzsche and Freud], the illusions that must be unmasked are those of self-interest masquerading as duty and virtue, and egoism pretending to the world and to itself that it is altruism. Nietzsche's example of the spirit resentment giving rise to a demand for revenge but posing as love and justice is a kind of paradigm. But sin is no more than selfishness *vis-a-vis* my neighbor. It is also the failure to love God with all my heart. Human self-deception now includes the will to autonomy from God alongside the will to dominance over my neighbor. Inevitably its introduction into the story adds the whole new dimension to the art of suspicion.[2]

Herein enters Nietzsche's departure from Kierkegaard while retaining his "art of suspicion." Rather than succumb to a moral system that leads to inevitable failure and misery (the Christian scheme), fomenting in *ressentiment* and hatred for others under the guise of "love" while plunging further and further into sickness to find "salvation" from the self that is supposedly created good

Jay Dyer

by God, Nietzsche turned Kierkegaard's suspicion on Christian morality itself, as well as upon the Enlightenment.

For Nietzsche, the Enlightenment had given rise to critique, or the art of suspicion, and in so doing, had tossed aside God. This is the origin of the famous "God is dead" phrase.[3] Rather than being a factual claim about what Nietzsche believed about some ontological scheme (as its often misinterpreted to mean), it's a descriptive statement about the current and future state of Western civilization and its relation to the Judeo-Christian God. The Enlightenment had successfully critiqued previous metaphysical and theological assumptions inherited from the likes of Plato, Aristotle, Galen, Ptolemy, Augustine, and Aquinas, only to find itself still seeking a grand narrative that amounted to the exaltation of an idealized and abstracted view of humankind. Immanuel Kant, for example, wrote that extrapolating a categorical moral imperative should logically lead to a world government where humanity is guided by reason and harmony—a veritable scientistic utopia! Yet, as we read Kierkegaard and then Nietzsche and Dostoevsky, we begin to see the problem with this abstraction.

Yet Descartes's *cogito, ergo sum* was not something Kierkegaard, Nietzsche, or Dostoevsky could completely avoid. The seeds of individualism had been laid. Descartes, himself somewhat of a rationalist, could not have foreseen the existential dilemma this idea would create, but his turning of humanity's gaze in on the self to deconstruct the psyche would result in the existentialists deconstructing the mythos of the Enlightenment. Twentieth-century Catholic philosopher Louis Dupré remarked:

> For Descartes, the truth of nature becomes established in the mind's reconstruction of it. The mind thereby functions as the mirror in whose reflection truth originates. But if so, how can it know itself, Gassendi wondered. The physical eye, incapable of seeing itself directly, nevertheless is

able to see itself in the mirror, yet for Descartes, there is no mirror beyond the mind. If we do not know the nature of the mirror, however, how can we evaluate its capacity for reflecting the true nature of things? In this objection lies the entire problem of knowledge as representation. Unless the eye know itself, how could it know how (and, in the end, what) it reflects? What allows the mind to refer the mirrored image to an original if it ignores how it reflects the original? Descartes felt that the objection went to the heart of his theory, and responded that the mind's mirror also reflects itself. Yet the mind possesses no more than an awareness of its existence. Does that suffice for justifying the knowledge of things in themselves through an act of representation? Locke perceived the difficulty and stated that the mind knows only its own ideas.[4]

Enlightenment thinking here began to collapse in on itself. It began to become evident that abstracted quantified measurement of all reality in a reductionist fashion—whether making all reality into matter or idea—ends in the same conundrum: solipsism. Solipsism is not the kind of position an Enlightenment rationalist would prefer to adopt since it is a fundamentally irrational position. Kierkegaard recognized that the self was dialectically related to itself and other selves and ultimately to the Other Self (God), and that its inability to find solace and meaning could be had in, so he thought, only a sort of individualistic justification by faith in the Lutheran scheme.

Nietzsche bit the bullet and simply rejected all of this in toto. In other words, why consider the self as evil as Christianity does? Why accept that God requires a debt that can be paid only by first recognizing our own inherent sinfulness? Didn't God know about humanity's infinite sinfulness to begin with? Thus the payment of an infinite death by sacrificing Himself to pay Himself becomes an exercise in irrationality. Yet Christianity, since the scholastic era, and its byproduct, the Enlightenment era, had been gradually arguing itself away from Christ's redemption into rationalism, and then by the same reasoning, rejecting rationalism by the arguments of reason itself. This quandary was not readily accepted by the deists and moralists of Nietzsche's time, yet Nietzsche was not afraid to call out the deists and scientists for their contradictions on their own grounds.

If the Enlightenment held the ontological reality that God was dead, then there was no coherent reason to hold onto Christian moralism, and in fact, these morals were themselves destructive and retrogressive to those who were strong. Christianity was slave morality par excellence as he argued in his two essays on the *Genealogy of Morals*, as well as in *Twilight of the Idols*, and *The Antichrist*. In fact, the entirety of Western civilization itself had started from false presuppositions that began with ascetics like Socrates and Plato who sought to flee the reality of the present into flights of fancy and abstractions. Plato gave the West a dialectical nightmare, and it would take people a few millennia to recover from it, if it could even be called a recovery. The modern atheistic scientists were no better; in fact, they were worse for arguing for something more contradictory than those in "Christendom." Nietzsche wrote three essays under the title "On the Genealogy of Morals: A Polemic Tract." In the third— "What Do Ascetic Ideals Mean?"—he took up the absurdity he saw in the so-called ascetics, which included the Enlightenment luminaries and the mediocre Germans of his own day.

For Nietzsche, the Enlightenment did cast off Christendom and its grand narrative that gave explanatory power to the seemingly random and harsh facts of life, but this was not an entirely lamentable fact. This removal of the idols of Bacon would be a tough pill to swallow. Indeed, it led to a kind of nihilism, as Dostoyevsky noted, but for Nietzsche this resulted in a possible rise of an artistic elite who would create a new meaning. Humanity's salvation would be found in art, and in aesthetics a new narrative and meaning might be presented. There was no determined necessity to this happening, of course. It was entirely possible that man might devolve, for progressive evolutionary theory is yet another Enlightenment myth: There is no law of progress present in the brute factuality of impersonal existence. For Nietzsche, this overman would bring redemption again—as the Antichrist because, in his analysis, Christianity was nihilism. He believed it was the Christian narrative and its inherent contradictions, resentment, and gradual degeneration that had led Western civilization to nihilism, and it was following upon this system's dissolution that a new man would arise.[5]

Twentieth-century American philosopher Robert Solomon explained:

> Aristotle had an ethos: Nietzsche leaves us with nothing. But Nietzsche is nevertheless the culmination of that whole tradition—which we still refer to as "moral philosophy" or "ethics"— which is based on a tragic and possibly irreversible error in both theory and practice. The error is the rejection of ethos as the foundation of morality with a compensating insistence on the rational justification of morality. Without a presupposed ethos, no justification is possible. Within an ethos, none is necessary. And so after centuries of degeneration, internal inconsistencies and failures in the Enlightenment project of transcending mere custom and justifying moral rules once and for all, the structures of morality have collapsed, leaving only incoherent fragments.[6]

Dostoevsky, however, remained a religious figure like Kierkegaard. A member of the Russian Orthodox tradition, in his younger years he was possessed by an optimistic, liberal view of human nature that would eventually morph into a more realistic, negative appraisal. In opposition to the classical liberal Western assumption that humanity can be raised up by education, and ever-more-complex education at that, Dostoevsky's writings give readers a window into the darker side of human nature that most would prefer to ignore and pretend doesn't exist. The Enlightenment's project, it must be recalled, was to tear away idols. Must not Western, hubris-filled people tear away this idol of the myth of his inward "goodness"? What of the inner darkness that results in atrocities? Why had the so-called progress of humanity resulted in ever-increasing warfare, upheaval, and revolution by Dostoyevsky's time? If people are not tabula rasa—blank slates upon which the correct imprinting by environment and education can create a harmonious, well-formed, mature individual—then what are they?

In *Notes from the Underground*, Dostoevsky gave a glimpse into the thoughts of a devious, vengeful, self-absorbed, slightly sadistic person. This petty person happened to be a typical person—a kind of everyman or everywoman, yet a highly intelligent one. The force of the literary presentation lies precisely in the fact that it is a person we all recognize, since his or her faults are common to all humans, yet this is a highly intelligent person. But if this kind of petty selfishness is present even in the most intelligent, seventeenth-century English philosopher John Locke's tabula rasa and that of the rest of the Enlightenment hopefuls and their idolized, abstracted smart humans simply replaced God with a new idol. Not only is there no abstracted scientist on a pedestal we can all aspire to; the fact is, most humans are petty, stupid, and not even capable of abstract reasoning. The ones who are generally are selfish and self-absorbed. Dostoyevsky's thinker mocked the idea that simply educating people and promoting "science" and "reason" would result in a better world:

> They say that Cleopatra (excuse an instance from
> Roman history) was fond of sticking gold pins into

her slave-girls' breasts and derived gratification from their screams and writhings. You will say that that was in the comparatively barbarous times; that these are barbarous times too, because also, comparatively speaking, pins are stuck in even now; that though man has now learned to see more clearly than in barbarous ages, he is still far from having learnt to act as reason and science would dictate. But yet you are fully convinced that he will be sure to learn when he gets rid of certain old bad habits, and when common sense and science have completely re-educated human nature and turned it in a normal direction. You are confident that then man will cease from *intentional* error and will, so to say, be compelled not to want to set his will against his normal interests. That is not all; then, you say, science itself will teach man (though to my mind it's a superfluous luxury) that he never has really had any caprice or will of his own, and that he himself is something of the nature of a piano-key or the stop of an organ, and that there are, besides, things called the laws of nature; so that everything he does is not done by his willing it, but is done of itself, by the laws of nature. Consequently we have only to discover these laws of nature, and man will no longer have to answer for his actions and life will become exceedingly easy for him. All human actions will then, of course, be tabulated according to these laws, mathematically, like tables of logarithms up to 108,000, and entered in an index; or, better still, there would be published certain edifying works of the nature of encyclopaedic lexicons, in which everything will be so clearly calculated and explained that there will be no more incidents or adventures in the world.

Then—this is all what you say—new economic relations will be established, all ready-made and worked out with mathematical exactitude, so that every possible question will vanish in the twinkling of an eye, simply because every possible answer to it will be provided. Then the "Palace of Crystal" will be built. Then ... In fact, those will be halcyon days. Of course there is no guaranteeing (this is my comment) that it will not be, for instance, frightfully dull then (for what will one have to do when everything will be calculated and tabulated), but on the other hand everything will be extraordinarily rational. Of course boredom may lead you to anything. It is boredom sets one sticking golden pins into people, but all that would not matter. What is bad (this is my comment again) is that I dare say people will be thankful for the gold pins then. Man is stupid, you know, phenomenally stupid; or rather he is not at all stupid, but he is so ungrateful that you could not find another like him in all Creation.[7]

In a brilliant turn of logic in literary form, Dostoevsky took Enlightenment thinkers to task for their scientism and rationalistic quantification as if human nature operated like an algorithm. It doesn't. Humans are irrational and stupid more often than not, and no amount of education and environmental alterations can cure flaws as simple as boredom, which often gives rise to bizarre, irrational behavior. No amount of education has been able to eradicate sadistic atrocities committed by people, following upon a few hundred years of the West adopting the new gospel of man given by the Enlightenment prophets. And in the greatest turn of absurdity, the very thing the Enlightenment set out to do—make reality rational to produce a better world—has ended up quantifying and reducing all reality to some monistic numerical tabulation of irrational, deterministic causation. This has resulted in the total denial of volition and will, absolutely. If all reality is a strict process of materialistic cause and effect, then free will is an illusion, and morals are thus also illusory. There can be no rational basis for morals on this assumption.

In conclusion, it becomes apparent that all three thinkers— Kierkegaard, Nietzsche, and Dostoevsky—contributed unique critical appraisals of the mythos of the Enlightenment. That mythos supposedly arose to give a primacy to human reason, the exaltation of science, the demythologization of superstition and religion, and the rise of "rational" and just international political structures. What actually occurred was the overturning of the previous Christian mythos that provided Western civilization with a cohesive grand narrative within which to situate the totality of existence. The collapse of this structure led immediately to the introspection of Kierkegaard and his dismal assessment of any hope of people finding themselves until first coming to the end of themselves and finding solace in the infinite God that transcends temporal, finite dialectics. For Nietzsche, the Enlightenment was yet another mythos that erected new idols in place of the old ones Bacon had supposedly torn down. Rigor in rationality, in fact, demanded that ethics be abandoned in favor of a new strong human arising who could create a new meaning. For Dostoevsky, the Enlightenment ate Christianity and then ate itself, exalting reason to the point of creating utterly unreal, idealistic assessments of humanity itself. The supposed gospel of man had resulted in a deterministic denial of humans that made the Enlightenment and its optimism impossible and absurd. And for Dostoevsky, as evidenced in *Crime and Punishment*, humanity would again have to come to the end of themselves, as Kierkegaard had foreseen, before finding redemption again.

Notes:

1   Francis Bacon, *Novum Organum* in *The Portable Enlightenment Reader*, ed. Isaac Kramnick (New York: Penguin, 1995), 39–42.

2   Merold Westphal, *Kierkegaard's Critique of Reason and Society* (Pennsylvania: Pennsylvania State University Press, 1987), 106.

3   Friedrich Nietzsche, *The Gay Science*, trans. Walter Kaufmann (New York: Random House, 1989), 191.

4   Louis Dupre, *Passage to Modernity: An Essay in the Hermeneutics of Nature and Culture* (New Haven: Yale University Press), 80.

5   Friedrich Nietzsche, "Genealogy of Morals: A Polemical Tract," essay 3: "What Do Ascetic Ideals Mean?" 95–6.

6   Robert Solomon, *Living With Nietzsche: What the Great "Immoralist" Has to Teach Us* (New York: Oxford, 2003), 128.

7   Fyodor Dostoyevsky, *Notes From the Underground* in *Basic Writings of Existentialism*, ed. Gordon Marino (New York: Random House, 2004), 213–14.

CHAPTER 7

Egyptian Mysteries of God and Energy ... I Will Show You a Great Mystery

> The Cosmos moves within the very life of eternity, and is contained in that very eternity whence all life issues. And for this reason it is impossible that it should at any time come to a standstill or be destroyed, since it is walled in and bound together, so to speak, by eternal life.[1]

Energy is not something pondered by most, yet energy is one of the most fundamental aspects of reality and figures prominently in physics, metaphysics, and theology. But what might a fundamental aspect of metaphysics have to do with geopolitics? Is there a correlation between energy and its process and social and political trends and movements? I think there is. Movement itself is energetic. All movement represents energy in motion, from one state of affairs to another. In theology we speak of God's active energies or attributes as the ultimate causation and ground of being in the universe, meaning energy itself is the locus of power. Speed also factors into this because speed is a certain rate of energetic action. Modernity has seen the increase of the speed of motion due to the advancement of technology: matter, information, and people are all able to move much faster and in much greater quantity than ever before.

Before considering questions of modern and future energy expectations, I would like to highlight an argument I've made a few times now concerning the ancient Egyptian hermetic notions and how their archetypal religious symbols encoded basic principles of quantum physics and the energetic process. As many esotericists and traditionalist thinkers have commented, it seems as if ages or eras of history also partake of cosmic processes or eons. Eastern writers speak of *kali yuga*, in which proper roles of hierarchy and caste are reversed. Twentieth-century German philosopher Oswald Spengler spoke of civilizations as having organic lifespans and Western humanity as "Faustian Man." My thesis here is that the cyclical process of energy itself gives a model of ages too. If movement is energetic, then history and time also reduce to energetic movement.

I have mentioned in the past that the rites of the gods encode secrets of nature. One of the best examples of this is the mythology of Isis, Apophis, and Osiris, whose mythology includes the principles of life and energy itself. Isis is the feminine principle of nature and energy extended in space and time, Apophis represents the principle of destruction and entropy, and Osiris represents the reemergence of energetic loss toward eternity to a higher state of eternality and immortality. The ancient Near Eastern symbol of IAO was representative of this formula, and when considered in comparison to the Pythagorean monad, dyad, and triad, the same imagery is found to encode the same formulae. The point or monad extends to the dyad, with the two points connected forming a line. The line either has a circumference drawn around it and/or extends to a third point. It can also form a vesica piscis, or an eye.

The eye is also a circle with a dot in the middle, as well as a circle surrounding a point or an extended line. This is the meaning of the obelisk in the circle, which, when viewed from above (as the gods would have seen it) is also a dot in a circle. Quantum physicist

Brian Greene discussed the fundamental energetic nature of reality as mirroring the binary computer model as follows:

> A datum that can answer a single yes-no question is called a bit—a familiar computer-age term that is short for binary digit, meaning a 0 or a 1, which you can think of as a numerical representation of yes or no … Notice that the value of the entropy and the amount of hidden information are equal. That's no accident. The number of possible heads-tail arrangements is the number of possible answers to the 1,000 questions—(yes, yes, no, no, yes, …) or (yes, no, yes, yes, no, …) … With entropy defined as the logarithm of the number of such arrangements—1,000 in this case—entropy is the number of yes-no questions any one such sequence answers … a system's entropy is the number of yes-no questions that its microscopic details have the capacity to answer, and so the entropy is a measure of the system's hidden information component … [in note] Stephen Hawking showed mathematically that the entropy of a black hole equals the number of Planck-sized cells that it takes to cover its event horizon. It's as if each cell covers one bit, one basic unit of information.[2]

At each point, there is being/energy, non-being, and again being. This fundamental pattern of energy is the fundamental pattern of energetic movement as well, as movement of objects is a transference of energy from one situation to another, as light itself encodes information. That is why the symbol for an open and closed energy current is the binary "I" and "O" combined to impede or allow the flow. The on/off symbol, as you see, is also the obelisk in the circle.

Thus, the entire process of nature and energy is contained in this one symbolic form. We don't have to be afraid of the "gods" or paganism in this regard, since all pagan exoteric religion has ever done is personalize or hypostatize the divine powers of God into chaotic, multiple powers (polytheism). These "natural forces" personified are energies of the One True God, not of countless demigods. To the inner priesthood of Egypt, the knowledge transmitted was that these gods were symbols for natural forces. In Egypt, symbols were magic, not representations of magic, and that is because the symbol participated in the "meaning" of the referent: the prototype participates in the archetype. This is so radically different a worldview from post-Enlightenment antimetaphysics and deconstructionism that it is very difficult for modern people to divest themselves of this assumption. Modernity assumes that symbols have no primeval, archetypal significance or meaning. Symbols and signs for modern people simply evolved at random from randomly evolved consciousness (whatever that is), which was then accepted in some kind of linguistic social contract when all the villagers decided, for example, that "cat" would stand for that little animal lying in the patch of sun on the rug.

Such are our great, learned academicians and professors. But to sober minds, the fundamental nature of energetic process also has a correspondence to civilizations and ages. Writer Mark Hackard has translated an excellent essay by Russian thinker Natalya Irtenina that describes the traditionalist assessment of our age, citing Guénon:

> Analyzing the worldview of the Middle Ages, one embodied in the aesthetic conception of Thomas Aquinas, the author Umberto Eco defines it as a "philosophy of cosmic order." In such an understanding of the world, "God is regarded as the *Prima Causa* in relation to Himself and to his Creation, for which he appears as the Actual, Final and Creative Reason … Here everything, beginning

> from the Creation of the angels, world and man, the
> determination of passions and habits, and ending
> in the sacraments as instruments of redemption
> and death as the gates to eternal life—none of this
> is accidental, all of this has its explanation and
> functions within this integral whole. [3]

At the base of what is called traditional consciousness or thinking lies the principle of hierarchy, strengthened by the idea of an absence of randomness, the impossibility of reasonless, acausal being. For the person located "within tradition," "all things have a traditional character since they are regarded in direct connection with foundational principles."[4]

I repeat these sufficiently simple and well-known truths here only to demonstrate the nucleus of logical relationships in the system of traditional thinking and from this to cross over to the topological plane of the given analysis. On the topological plane, the integrity of traditional thinking is structured according to the principle of the tree: the roots (basic metaphysical principles), the trunk (the One, the highest level of hierarchy), and the widely branching crown (the *universum* of the Cosmos, particularly human culture). Within the parameters of modern scientific rationalism (in the projects of philosophers, linguists, semioticians, structuralists, psychologists, psychiatrists, and certain polymaths), the tree principle has already long been legitimized as an epistemological, methodological reality, as an archetype, and in general as "one of the strongest 'universal' structures of man's thought and practice in apprehending the world."

The reference to tradition here is crucial, as meaning can be had only in a certain context, just as words having meaning only in a certain context, just as stories have meanings only in a certain context. Modernity is premised on the new as new. But nothing can be truly new in the sense that the modernists and nihilists want. The overwhelming sense of boredom and bondage engendered by liberalism from the time of the Enlightenment on is a result of this impossible, erotic desire for the purely new. This desire for the continually new is actually modernity's slavery, despite its false assumption that it is its greatest freedom. The "new" is where the past is supposedly discarded, and atomized individual meaningless "consciousness" creates its own meaning and foists it upon the world as the direct result of liberalism's inherent nihilism. Russian geo-strategist Alexander Dugin brilliantly summed up this nihilistic impulse of modern liberalism as follows:

> There is one point in liberal ideology that has brought about a crisis within it: liberalism is profoundly nihilistic at its core. The set of values defended by liberalism is essentially linked to its main thesis: the primacy of liberty. But liberty in the liberal vision is an essentially negative category: it claims to be free from (as per John Stuart Mill), not to be free for something. It is not secondary; it is the essence of the problem.

> Liberalism fights against all forms of collective identity, and against all types of values, projects, strategies, goals, methods and so on that are collectivist, or at least non-individualist. That is the reason why one of the most important theorists of liberalism, Karl Popper (following Friedrich von Hayek), held in his important book, *The Open Society and Its Enemies*, that liberals should fight against any ideology or political philosophy (ranging from Plato and Aristotle to Marx and Hegel) that suggests that human society should have some common goal, common value, or common meaning. (It should be noted that George Soros regards this book as his personal bible.) Any goal, any value, and any meaning in liberal society,

or the open society, should be strictly based upon the individual. So the enemies of the open society, which is synonymous with Western society post-1991, and which has become the norm for the rest of the world, are concrete. Its primary enemies are Communism and fascism, both ideologies which emerged from the same Enlightenment philosophy, and which contained central, non-individualistic concepts—class in Marxism, race in National Socialism, and the national State in fascism. So the source of liberalism's conflict with the existing alternatives of modernity, fascism or Communism, is quite obvious. Liberals claim to liberate society from fascism and Communism, or from the two major permutations of explicitly non-individualistic modern totalitarianism. Liberalism's struggle, when viewed as a part of the process of the liquidation of non-liberal societies, is quite meaningful: it acquires its meaning from the fact of the very existence of ideologies that explicitly deny the individual as society's highest value. It is quite clear what the struggle is attempting to achieve: liberation from its opposite. But the fact that liberty, as it is conceived by liberals, is an essentially negative category is not clearly perceived here. The enemy is present and is concrete. That very fact gives liberalism its solid content. Something other than the open society exists, and the fact of its existence is enough to justify the process of liberation.[5]

In other words, liberal modernity post Enlightenment has lost all conception of birth and nature, and resurrection and eternality. There is only the futile thrust for the ever new, which represents a vain grasping for the "O" (Osiris) while being perpetually enmeshed in the "A" (Apophis and entropy). The acceptance of Darwinian theory itself by all of modernity is nothing but the acceptance of the principle of perpetual chaos and entropy. Although early Darwinian progressives assumed humans were evolving into more and more progressive states, once it becomes evident that progress (in that worldview) is a subjective value judgment with no objective reality, the concept is meaningless (as is everything). The jettisoning of metaphysics by the Enlightenment, exaltation of the atomized individual, and apotheosis of the new is simply to be caught forever in the cyclical wheel of natural chaos. It is the implicit worship of Apophis, and is, as Dugin said, pure nihilism.

In terms of geopolitics, the Western elite have come to embody the full incarnation of what Spengler correctly described as Faustian. Johann Wolfgang von Goethe's nineteenth-century fictitious Dr. Faustus (based on a real character) made a deal with the devil for power, but as a result lost himself and his soul. What better description for Western humanity than Faustian, given the insane, nihilistic goals of technological transhumanism in a universe simultaneously divested of any meaning or significance as a result of modern liberalism, where this nihilistic tech-utopia version seeks to attain immortality through a mass Creation of chaos (Apophis). But the process of IAO, if it does have any historical connection, is not caused and created by power-mad technocrats who wreck everything thinking they will remake everything. That is the folly of communistic metaphysics—order out of chaos. Suicide does not make for immortality.

Irtenina commentted again:

> If the model of traditional thought can be signified by the letter **Ψ** (everything grows out of and is nourished by a single trunk), then the neo-pagan model will look like a **Ψ** inverted (of course both definitions are quite conditional). In the latter case, although subordination of the system's elements

to the "one" is distinctly obvious, the space of the *Universum* unfolds not in the crown of the tree, but in the ramified system of roots. The culture of this "Brave New World" is steeped in the militant heritage of a pagan past bursting upon the present scene and sweeping away all in its path.[6]

The inverted Greek *psi*, an inverted tree, also resembles a pyramid, as does the A of Apophis (which actually embodies the uncapped pyramid). The triadic pyramid itself is not evil, but when inverted is symbolic of evil, the negation of being. The reality is that nothing is truly new because nothing is relative. No meaning is purely contingent that suddenly emerges as a brute fact in history with no historical context. But objects in history are also not purely historical and subject to constant flux. History itself is contained within the infinite, as every point in space and time also manifests the infinite, as I showed here. And that means truth itself is also eternal, not temporal and meaningless. In short, the entire universe is the opposite of what the Faustian degenerate Western so-called "elite" have proffered. Apophis is not the ultimate force in the universe, but merely an aberration that marks temporal reality itself. Apophis and entropy cannot be universalized and apotheosized because they are not things—they have no being. They are the negation of being, being no-thing. The nothingness of nihilism is the very thing liberalism tends toward as twentieth-century Russian political philosopher Aleksandr Dugin accurately noted.

In terms of geopolitics, the race of modernity centers around energy. The fiat dollar is itself a symbolic representation of human energy. To bind all the world to a fiat currency of ones and zeros in a computer grid is to enslave humankind to a central, virtual grid of nihilistic monetarism. Most nations in the world use the same fraudulent central banking model that we have here in the United States—the Federal Reserve model based in turn on the Bank of England model. The binding of masses to a single binary electronic "currency" thus encapsulates the transference of human energy into virtual energy, yet it is a system that is even more susceptible to centralized fraud and manipulation than the older fiat paper models. It is therefore the liberal, nihilistic negation of currency and "money" (for the masses, that is). Our era of reign of quantity and monetarism is perfectly summarized with an Apophis *A* on the "dollar."

With these deep ruminations in mind, the context of the Anglo-establishment's war on Russia for the last hundred years represents a race for energy. The Anglo elites, enmeshed in satanism and their Faustian tech bargain, have adopted wholesale the lie that the control of natural resources, and in particular energy, will give them not merely some classical geopolitical advantage, but rather immortality. This immortality will (they believe) be achieved by the utter dominance and cutting off of natural resources. The complete and total control of energy, in all forms and means, is the essence of full spectrum dominance. It is not merely the control of natural gas, coal, nuclear energy, or emergent energy technologies—it is the control of all movement. All movement is energy as I have noted, and the tracking and tracing of all things is merely another example of full-spectrum energy dominance. Control of currency is control of energy. Control of food is control of the consumption of energy. Control of breeding is control of sexual energy. The name of the entire game is cornering the market on energy—*all energy*. This is the meaning of the evil, Apophis version of the eye. The palantír-style magic crystal ball that is the Internet and Google *is* the ring of power—or the ring of *energy*. But the ring of energy does not end with entropy and Apophis. It ends with resurrection and immortality, and that is a symbolic reassurance and guarantee that the forces of destruction, chaos, and Apophis will not, and cannot, win in the long run. A is also Alpha and O is also Omega.

God transcends the dualist metaphysic exemplified in nature and the energetic process. Eastern theologian Vladimir Lossky explains:

"According to St. Maximus, God is 'identically a monad and a triad.'" *Capita theologica et oeconomica* 2, 13; P.G. 90, col. 1125A. He is not merely one and three; he is 1=3 and 3=1. That is to say, here we are not concerned with number as signifying quantity: absolute diversities cannot be made the subjects of sums of addition; they have not even opposition in common. If, as we have said, a personal God cannot be a monad — if he must be more than a single person — neither can he be a dyad. The dyad is always an opposition of two terms, and, in that sense, it cannot signify an absolute diversity. When we say that God is Trinity we are emerging from the series of countable or calculable numbers. St. Basil appears to express this idea well: "For we do not count by way of addition, gradually making increase from unity to plurality, saying 'one, two, three' or 'first, second, third.' 'I am the first and I am the last,' says God (Isaiah 44:6). And we have never, even unto our own days, heard of a second God. For in worshipping 'God of God' we both confess the distinction of persons and abide by the Monarchy." *De spiritu sancto* 18; P.G. 32, col. 149B. The procession of the Holy Spirit is an infinite passage beyond the dyad, which consecrates the absolute (as opposed to relative) diversity of the persons. This passage beyond the dyad is not an infinite series of persons but the infinity of the procession of the Third Person: the Triad suffices to denote the Living God of revelation. St. Gregory of Nazianzus, *Or.* 23 (*De pace* 3), 10; P.G. 35, col. 1161. *Or.* 45 (*In sanctum pascha*); P.G. 36, col. 628C. If God is a monad equal to a triad, there is no place in him for a dyad. Thus the seemingly necessary opposition between the Father and the Son, which gives rise to a dyad, is purely artificial, the result of an illicit abstraction. Where the Trinity is concerned, we are in the presence of the One or of the Three, but never of two.[7]

Notes:

1   (Asclepius III, 29c.)
2   (*The Hidden Reality*, 289-290)
3   (Eco, "Aesthetics of the Chaosmos")
4   (Guénon)
5
6
7

CHAPTER 8

Numbers Refute Materialism

Twentieth-century American philosopher Thomas Nagel recently published a book questioning the hallowed dogma of strict, reductionist materialism. I have not read the book, but a philosopher friend recommended it to me. It's nice to see someone daring to challenge the ridiculous control grid that is modern so-called academia. In a similar vein this week, a friend set up a Google chat in which I was able to meet an MIT professor and debate certain questions relating to materialism and Platonism. While I have to tread lightly here, I want to make it clear that I am not advocating everything Plato taught; however, in the course of debating academics and thinkers, appeals to the hallowed tradition of Platonism and mathematics seem to have some weight as an inroad. I don't think I made much progress in my discussion with the MIT chap, but it illustrates for me further confirmation of the correctness of my own positions on metaphysics.

In the course of this conversation, several ideas came to mind that highlight the impossibility of rank materialism. I have highlighted many of them here already, but it's always good to revisit them, since modernity is so committed to this dogma without question.

The first faulty presupposition is naive empiricism. The scientific and academic establishments are still dominated by naive empiricism as a sole epistemological approach. Believe anything you want, in fact, just as long as undergirding all of it is the ridiculous idea that all knowledge comes through sense experience. This is the ancient error of the sophists, nominalists, and Enlightenment empiricists.

Caught up in the populist ideas of their times, these philosophers and thinkers simply assume that the intellectual climate that fostered progress was found only in circles that adhered to this doctrine. Nothing could be further from the truth. Since most members of this school follow some form of what they would term logic, it is very easy to demonstrate that the claim "all knowledge comes through sense experience" is false by appealing to the sentence itself. The claim is an exceptionally strong universal claim about both knowledge and metaphysics. Given the propensity of these people to bully theists for unsubstantiated claims, there is no possible way, on empirical grounds, to prove such a claim. The claim itself necessarily entails an entire host of metaphysical preconditions, too, which are anathema to naive empiricism. Even twentieth-century American philosopher Willard Van Orman Quine, one of their own, showed that the very dogmatic claim of naive empiricism is an impossible claim and is still quite impossible. In fact, you can read David Hume himself, the grandfather of modern atheistic materialism, for an elaborate explanation of how empiricism necessarily entails radical skepticism and is therefore utterly destructive to all knowledge. For example, in a piece in the American political magazine *The Weekly Standard* on Nagel's recent workshop with materialists, we read:

> At the workshop the philosophers and scientists each added his own gloss to neo-Darwinian reductive naturalism or materialistic neo-Darwinian reductionism or naturalistic materialism or reductive determinism. They were unanimous in their solid certainty that materialism—as we'll call it here, to limit the number of isms—is the all-purpose explanation for life as we know it.[1]

Since modern academia is not much more than a vast machine of brainwashing and propaganda, we cannot expect much, but as with most "educated intellectuals," knowledge of Plato rarely consists of more than a smattering of *The Republic* and a few dialogues. My concern here is not to delve into Plato's theory of the polis, but to highlight the metaphysics. Modern academia being the machine it is, adherents know only to follow the popular line of Plato as this, that, or the other, and almost never hit on the fact that Plato was part of an esoteric tradition extending from Egypt and older cultures that had a specific cosmogony and cosmology that closely connected with anthropology embodied in the classic microcosm-macrocosm analogy.

Since my opponents were not familiar with the *Timaeus*, we were at a bit of a loss because the *Timaeus* exemplifies this tradition so clearly. I am not saying that all the statements about polytheism or Creation by the gods are necessarily metaphysically correct or literal; I do believe that there is a great amount of truth in the work that clearly extends back to an older Creation tradition that is very similar to the Mosaic in which the logos or word is preeminent in the Creation act. This means the external world,—whatever "stuff" we conceive it to be made of—is inherently rational and imbued with meaning and the manifestation of the divine *energeia*. The modern materialists hold the utmost opposite as their working presupposition: meaning and logos are merely social conventions foisted upon reality from finite, meaningless brains that resulted from equally meaningless materialistic process. On the contrary, what I further realized in the course of the conversation was how vastly different were our approaches to the world as a whole. My operating presuppositions so radically differed in my view of the world that it was very difficult to translate them into concepts that even make some kind of sense for the diehard materialist.

My next argument after criticizing empiricism was the classic one relating to numbers, which all materialists find difficulty grasping. Let's take a logical entity like the number seven. Consider that collecting seven objects alone cannot account for the invariant, unchanging, and eternal conceptual nature of something like seven. We can begin to see that a number proper is not like material things in a very fundamental way. In other words, the classic philosophical problem of identity and predication emerges as something impossible for rank materialism. What is a number if it is clearly not a mere collection of these atoms? Even if the materialist affirms that "seven" is just the collection of some seven objects, it begs the question: is that *particular* collection *the* number seven? Clearly not, since the removal of one of the objects does not suddenly erase the number seven from existence. I apologize to more thoughtful readers that such basic philosophy has to still be recounted, since anyone who has taken philosophy 101 knows this is one of the first things discussed. Consider another illustration: which is *the* number seven?

Seven

VII

7

IIIIIII

The answer is all and none. This is the problem of the one and the many, a very dastardly problem for rank materialists. Seven—the conceptual reality—is therefore something that transcends each of these concrete particular symbolic representations. The pure materialists must always, of necessity, reduce all conceptual reality to some arbitrary collection of the molecules and atoms and arbitrarily predicate "sevenness" to those things. But if all reality is mere matter, the brains engaged in the process of predicating seven do not contain the same neural impulses that are firing to cause the concept seven. So the question can be reframed as follows: in the collection of numbers in the list I've included here, what is it that causes us to connect these different symbols? What, precisely, is the nature of the connectedness? It cannot be simply what is happening in our minds chemically because we are looking for the connecting principle or meaning behind these events. The chemicals in my head are not the chemicals in yours, so what is sevenness? Simply restating it as those molecules and these molecules begs the question, since assuming that the mind can pick out a certain collection of molecules as a specific object of predication just assumes materialism again. It is as if to say, "signs and symbols have no real ontological status beyond being token symbols of material reality because the chemical reactions in the brain that equate to being signs and symbols." But this is logical and philosophical nonsense.

While I do not fully agree with twentieth-century Swedish-American physicist Max Tegmark that all reality is purely math, he is definitely on the right track when he talks about how the fundamental nature of reality is quite different from what these people imagine. Rather than adopting the ridiculous and childish idea that mathematics is an invention of human social construct, Tegmark explains that mathematics is very much at the heart of reality and very much something that precedes humankind. In contrast to the materialists and existentialists who hold that existence precedes essence, the worldview I espouse is quite the opposite: essence precedes human existence. Meaning and number are not random Creations of chaotic process; they are the very fabric of reality itself and are not dependent on the "invention" of some guy.

When we read the *Timaeus*, we see that, even at that early date, Pythagoras, Socrates, and Plato had a conception that the fundamental structure of reality was based around geometry—the very archetypal forms of nature. In authentic education taught in the trivium and quadrivium, we know that geometry is number in space while music is number in time. Through the *Timaeus*, we can see that, early in this tradition, there was an almost magical conception of the idea that, at a very fundamental level, reality is geometrically structured into forms known now as the Platonic solids. We can see these forms in everything in our world from the molecular level to the cosmic level. The Platonic solids follow upon the pattern of the one, the dyad, and triad, which extend out to make all geometrical shaped and forms. These structures emerge everywhere in nature and show that all reality is highly structured and ordered, as opposed to being the product of random chaotic forces. For example, by the use of cymatics we can see that notes in music have a certain form when played on a surface that can demonstrate the geometrical structure they produce.

Only a fool would think that the platonic solids have chemical equivalents by random happenstance. On the contrary, these things demonstrate very clearly that we are right as positing an omniscient mind as the source of all these interconnected phenomena. We see this more clearly when we examine the notions of linguistic philosophy and the problem of predication, which I have outlined elsewhere. It also shows that reality itself has its own metaphysical structure that functions as a precondition for even the possibility of knowledge at all in a transcendental sense. By transcendental here, I am referring to transcendental philosophy and not anything else.

From this point in the conversation, I went on to argue that the very possibility of creating an AI supercomputer or something like the cloud assumes a world far different from what the materialists imagine. This sounds a bit odd at first glance, since, generally speaking, it's the AI fanatics and tech geeks who are often the first to cry that computing so loudly heralds the dawn of the victory of the materialist worldview. On the contrary again, the ability to encode information in light, based on the fact that light itself is information, is precisely proof of the opposite of what these fools believe. The ability to store information in a sort of realm of forms, if you will, in which algorithms and sets stand for reality is an analogy of what must be the case on a more cosmic, interdimensional level. There are two reasons that we cannot locate the essence of things solely in the concrete historical of a thing. First, there is the problem of the one and many I outlined above. Second, there is the classical philosophical problem of identity over time. This does not mean that someone who takes the route I am mentioning de facto has all answers to all questions either. But if our starting points lead us to the utmost absurdities, as raw materialism does, it must be jettisoned for real progress to occur.

I often reference twentieth-century American logician and philosopher Kurt Gödel because the incompleteness theorem is a great example of why no system can be explained solely by the axioms that undergird the system. Gödel showed this against Bertrand Russell's challenge, yet many people are unable to make the connections as to what the implications of this are. Not only does it show that mathematical sets cannot be justified by reference to other mathematical sets, as the book *Gödel, Escher, Bach: An Eternal Golden Braid* shows, this pattern emerges in other disciplines and areas of life. But even twentieth-century American scholar of cognitive science and physics Douglas Hofstadter cannot seem to make the connection between this and why materialism is false. As I mentioned with regard to Gödel, a friend sent me an interesting piece the other day that appears to be true and confirms something he and I had been speculating about lately: is there something more sinister at work in terms of the suppression of Platonism and the promotion of rank materialism? Readers of my blog will know that I certainly think the promotion of communistic dialectical materialism is demonstrably true and conspiratorial, but is there a flipside to this idea in which the truth about the actual nature of reality is being suppressed? Perceptive readers and friends will recall that I have made mention in the past of my suspicion that there is much more to Leibniz and to Husserl in particular than is commonly known, and what my friend sent me especially perked my ears.

Apparently, I am not the first to wonder about this idea. A blogger recently put together a fascinating article about Gödel coming to the same conclusion regarding the actual philosophical tradition we are now taught in the West. And whom did Gödel specifically pick as suppressed? He fingered two Platonists—Leibniz and Husserl. The blog reads:

> Perhaps the greatest logician of all time, Kurt Gödel uncovered the existence of a world-wide conspiracy to make men less intelligent. For years Gödel had been very interested in the work of Gottfried Leibniz, whose characteristica universalis influenced Gödel's use of symbolism in his famous incompleteness proofs, and went so far as to request copies of the voluminous Leibniz manuscripts to be brought to the United States during the second World War. Gödel initially claimed to have discovered evidence of a conspiracy suppressing Leibniz's work— that Leibniz had in fact completed the famously unfinished (and unfinishable) universal language of thought, but had been prevented from publishing it. In conversation, Gödel suggested that the Viennese Academy of Science, officially inaugurated in the mid-19th century, had in fact been founded by Leibniz in secret some centuries before; its record books, which contained references to the complete *characteristica universalis*, had been systematically destroyed.[2]

And a commenter wrote:

> I came across this in *On the Philosophical Development of Kurt Gödel* Author(s): Mark Van Atten and Juliette Kennedy on page 452-453 in a footnote: "[After quoting Gödel talking about a manuscript of Husserl that had been removed from published record] Gödel has made similar remarks about manuscripts disappearing, e.g., some of

Leibniz', which have sometimes been dismissed as symptoms of a possible mental instability on Gödel's part. But in this case, Gödel was completely correct, and by way of proof he pointed Sue Toledo [92, p.9] So we have here another case of Gödel's allegations of important works being removed actually being evidence of his meticulous research abilities.[3]

This is both amazing and important. There is a *characteristica universalis* because Plato was right. Of course I cannot verify if this is absolutely correct, but it is something I have spoken to others about for a few years now. My intuition is almost always right. These last facts about Gödel do not prove anything about the case against the materialist, but they do fit perfectly into why I think we will eventually win out in the long run against the materialist enemies and haters of truth. Because the world is actually so far from what they think, their "system" cannot win out in the long run. Anything at odds with actual reality can only fail in the long march of history. True, Plato argued with the sophists of his day, and Leibniz did battle with the materialists of his, but in our day, things are coming to a head. The big discoveries in theoretical physics are starting to vindicate our view of reality as opposed to the chaos philosophers of nonsense. They fail to realize that they war against their own very being and *logoi* and are thus doomed to fail. The solution to this dilemma is the notion of a single unified science, as Dr. Phillip Sherrard accurately explained in his essay "A Single Unified Science."

Notes:

1   Imannuel Kant, *Critique of Pure Reason* (Buffalo, New York: Prometheus Books, 1990), 478–9.
2   Aristotle. *Metaphysics, Bk. M 13* in *The Basic Works of Aristotle*, ed. Richard McKeon (New York: Random House, 1941), 888.

3   Ibid., 889.

4   Ibid., 892.

5   Michael J. White, "The Metaphysical Location of Aristotle's 'Mathematika,'" *Phronesis* Vol. 38. No. 2 (1993): 166–8.6 Ibid., 893.

6

7   Ibid., 731.

8   Ibid., 691-2.

9   Jonathan Barnes, "Metaphysics" in *The Cambridge Companion to Aristotle* (New York: Cambridge University Press, 1995), 92.

10 Aristotle, *Metaphysics*, 911.

11 On the centrality of mathematics to the Pythagoreans, see John Burnet, *Greek Philosophy: Thales to Plato* (London: MacMillan and Co., 1964), 40–44.

12 Aristotle, *Metaphysics,* Bk 1, 691.

13 Plato, *Timaeus* in *Collected Dialogues* (Princeton, New Jersey: Princeton University Press, 1961), 1156–7.

14 Plato. *Critias*, 1214–15.

15 *Timaeus*, 1168–9.

16 See *Metaphysics*, Bk. 12, Ch. 8–9.

17 Stefan Wimmer, "Hieroglyphics—Writing and Literature" in *Egypt: The World of the Pharaohs* (China: Tandem Verlag GmbH, 2007), 343.

18 *Timaeus*, 1156-7.

19 James B. Pritchard, *The Ancient Near East Vol. 1: An Anthology of Texts and Pictures* (New Jersey: Princeton University Press, 1958), 1.

20 Ibid., 1.

21 For more on the importance of Thoth in Egyptian conceptions of divine speech, see Egyptologist Wim van den Dungen, "To Become a Magician: the Sacred Great Word, its Divine Record by the Ante-rational Mind and the Magic of the Everlasting Existence of Pharaoh's Life-Light. *Sofiatopia.org.* Retrieved August, 2011, http://www.sofiatopia.org/maat/heka.htm

22 Wim van den Dungen, "Hermes the Egyptian." Retrieved August, 2011, http://www.sofiatopia.org/maat/hermes1.htm

23 Wim van den Dungen, "Ancient Egyptian Roots of the Principia Hermetica." Retrieved on August, 2011, http://www.sofiatopia.org/maat/ten_keys.htm

24 Ibid.

25 Lisa Randall, *Warped Passages: Unraveling the Mysteries of the Universes Hidden Dimensions* (New York: Harper Collins, 2005).

26 Ibid., 4–5.

27 Brian Greene, *The Hidden Reality: Parallel Universes and the Deep laws of the Cosmos* (New York: Vintage Books, 2011), 289–90.

28 Piet Hut, Mark Alford, and Max Tegmark, "On Math, Matter and Mind," *Foundations of Physics*. October 20, 2005, http://arxiv.org/PS_cache/physics/pdf/0510/0510188v2.pdf

29

30

31

CHAPTER 9

Leibniz Plus John Dee = Golems

I have written before about the importance of sixteenth/seventeenth-century German polymath and Platonist, Gottfried Leibniz, especially when it comes to complex metaphysical questions. Some have wondered in the past why I have seen him as important, and I want to explain what I began to notice several years ago. This is not to say that I think all his ideas are correct. Indeed, several of his ideas seem a bit strange, but there are definitely crucial insights and ideas handed down in the Western tradition that Leibniz brought to light and that ultimately led to the computational machine we call the computer. Certainly others were involved in this long process, such as Blaise Pascal in the seventeenth century and other mathematicians, but Leibniz occupies a central role.

As readers of my website (https://jaysanalysis.com/) may have noticed, my interview with James Kelley, author of *Anatomyzing Divinity: Studies in Science, Esotericism, and Political Theology*, highlighted several questions surrounding figures of that era speculating on optics and the ability to influence people and nations for propaganda and psychological operations purposes. Specifically, Dr. John Dee, seventeenth-century English mathematician, astronomer, and alchemist, theorized different notions about magical mirrors that might be erected to influence others. James Kelley offered the tantalizing idea that the two zeroes in the "007" symbolism Dee used in his communiques with Queen Elizabeth I may have represented two mirrors placed as they would have been in the optical experiments of his day. And the seven represented the point of light reflecting outward. Kelley mentioned that Dee theorized that the universe was a vast body of luminous light that corresponded to the androgynous Adam Kadmon of Jewish Kabbalistic lore, and the light in the eyes of human beings was the means by which the rays that refracted off objects could thus transmit the emblems of information and knowledge into our heads.

Much needs to be said here. This theory is very close to Aristotle's view that the mind abstracts universals from the phantasm. These enter the mind through sense experience. In similar fashion, Enlightenment theorists, including the esotericists, were fascinated by these notions as well as the Platonic illuminist theory of epistemology that Augustine supported. Ron Nash has written an interesting book contrasting the Augustinian and Thomistic conceptions of knowledge, with Thomas following Aristotle in the great synthesis more than Plato, though Aquinas did think he had synthesized the two by placing the archetypes of forms of things in the divine essence. In this regard, Augustine's illuminism is very similar to that of Aquinas, as both sought to base human knowledge on the reflected analogies that are in people's minds that lead them to a contemplative journey back to the One.

For both Aquinas and Augustine, the archetypes or forms of things that are in the divine essence become a kind of mental path converts must make as they are led through life on the perilous quest to see the true nature of things in God. Yet the fatal flaw that the East elucidates here is that the goal of this quest is to find the essence of God. For Aquinas and Augustine, the foundation of natural and supernatural knowledge was the illuminating grace God gives to see the true forms of things in the absolutely simple divine essence. Thus, for both theologians, the divine essence is literally spoken of as a kind of mirror of reality that the mind of humanity refracts, leading people from the creaturely analogies back to the true forms in the essence of the One, the divine essence of God, synonymous with the Divine Mind.

This is divine exemplarism, but with a unique twist that distinguishes the Western view from the Eastern: Maximus the Confessor placed these archetypes or logoi as energies of God in the one logos, not as the divine essence. This has crucial implications for theology, but in terms of my focus here, there are massive implications for epistemology. James Kelley has laid out many of these implications in his book, but as he mentioned in our interview, there appear to be interesting parallels with the track of Western civilization as its top ancient scientists and philosophers like Bacon, Leibniz, Descartes, Dee, and Newton take this alchemical-Platonic view of "trinities" everywhere and reverse engineer them into a technological idea of a great god computer, if you will.

For many Renaissance and Enlightenment thinkers, the mind was a mirror of the world, capable of "imaging" anything in the world, and following the Platonic and Aristotelian theories of illumination, in a sense potentially infinite. The form of any single thing can enter the mind through the eye, be stored in the mind, and be reproduced via memory. Thus, for many of these thinkers, not only does it appear they had a mechanistic view of humanity as their presupposition for the scientific revolution, but a more esoteric notion of creating a computing machine. With the assumption of humans as sort of biological machines, it was thus posited that a mechanical being might be created.

Readers will immediately think of the ancient Kabbalistic legend of the Golem, the mechanical man that can be created with the proper symbols and magic. In the sixteenth century, Rabbi Isaac of Luria supposedly created one, being a master of the Kabbalistic arts. However, rather than pass away into the bin of history as an unknown myth, I suspect that, in the esoteric societies of Dee and Leibniz and company, the myth persisted, and when these were combined with the other theories of Augustino-platonic illuminism, Augustinian epistemic mirror emblemism, and so forth, the stage was set for the proposal of concepts that would evolve into the complex computing systems we now have. In this book, I want to analyze some of the ideas of Gottfried Leibniz. We know that he was the founder of calculus, and particularly of theories that would be instrumental for the Creation of the computer, but were there esoteric ideas beyond mere mathematics at work? Do the concepts of mirror imaging and reflecting, the monadology, space and extension in Leibniz demonstrate any possible connection to what we see before us in these complex instruments known as personal computers? What about the ideas that Dr. John Dee had, as James Kelley has noted, served to influence later scientists to create great eyes in the sky that could peer anywhere and also project images everywhere, propagandizing masses?

Leibniz was interested in finding a *characteristica universalis*, a universal language of symbols—a universal lexicon that would represent all the functions of reason. The idea here would eventually evolve into the Creation of the computer—a "logic machine" that could perform complex algorithms. While machines might be created to count (primitive calculators), what about more complex machines that could encode data? Could that data be stored? Though I am not schooled in the history of technology, I am a student of philosophy, and the question does pique my interest. We would be told by most modern-day technicians and scientists that pure materialist trial and error was the birthplace of these techno marvels we now see, but I suspect this is false. I am much more inclined to believe that behind these "logic machines" are vast metaphysical speculations as well as profound metaphysical truths.

Readers will also notice that I have often referred generally to the "Platonic tradition" as more correct than the empirical tradition, and it is worth noting that Leibniz certainly embraced that strand of thought. I am not advocating rationalism here, or "Platonism," but I do suggest that core ideas in that tradition stand in stark contrast to the materialist and empirical traditions that dominate our world to this day. Indeed, as I mentioned, most computer scientists likely posit that computers emerged from a long process of materialistic, scientistic endeavor. Yet when we look at Leibniz, we do not see someone enveloped in materialism and mechanistic views of the world, but rather someone who embraces an elaborate scholastic worldview that hearkens to Platonism.

Leibniz's monadology is his metaphysical theory of reality being composed of infinite, rational, simple monads that function like a little spherical mirror. The monads mirror the rest of reality but do not directly interact with one another. God has pre-established a perfect harmony between them, and it is correct to say that, properly speaking, the monads are spirit as opposed to matter. Leibniz rejected the idea that fundamental reality was made up of material atoms; he posited instead that mind, particularly the Divine Mind, was the ground of reality manifest in all the infinite monads. In this theory, Leibniz actually presages many twentieth-century developments in quantum physics, including the theories of Wolfgang Pauli and psychiatrist Carl Jung regarding the continuity of the inner concepts of the psyche and the outer archetypes encountered in the world of physics. For Jung, psyche—or mind—bridged that gap, and Leibniz would agree, arguing that reality is, at base, conscious. I also see similarity between Maximus the Confessor and his logoi. For all these thinkers, reality was grounded in the mind of God, though they differ quite a bit in what that entails and how that is.

Twentieth-century American philosopher Philip Weiner explained in my copy of Leibniz's works (*Leibniz Selections*):

> Monads come into existence as "fulgurations" or sparks of the divine, falling within the limits of pre-established harmony. They are spiritual, rather than physical points ... Each monad is graded according to its powers of mental activity, the higher monad perceiving changes within itself more clearly, distinctly, or adequately than the lower ones, and in

so doing, "mirrors" more of the objective relations of the entire universe of monads from its point of view. The ensemble of these points of view forms an order of co-existence, and space is nothing but the simultaneous perception of co-existing qualities, and time is nothing but the order of successively perceived qualities. The spaces and times of each monad will be relative to the point of view of each.

The inherent effort of each essence to realize the maximum existence is the metaphysical basis for Leibniz's defense of a spontaneous freedom of the will ... in the case of each individual men's essences ... The ultimate individuals (monads) of the universe are then active centers of energy containing all that they have been or will be within themselves."[1]

Unfortunately, Leibniz was still working within the context of the Augustino-Platonic tradition, which defined God as an absolutely simple monad, all of whose attributes and actions are conceived of as wholly synonymous with that divine essence. God is the exact same as what He does. This is the classic Western doctrine of divine simplicity from the time of Augustine on, but to be fair to Leibniz, he does consider God as the Great monad to be of a different order than the rest of reality, though still part of that continuum in the Great Chain of Being, since the monads all mirror the Great Simple monad.

Leibniz wrote in his *First Principles: Foundations of the Sciences*: "The most Perfect Being is the one that contains the most of essence. Quality is being, capable of having ideas and reflections, for this multiplies the variety of things as a mirror does."[2]

Leibniz's only book to be published in his lifetime was *Theodicy* in which he attempted to make sense of the problem of evil. However, that is not my interest here; I want to focus on his metaphysics. In the section "Identity in Individuals and True Propositions," he wrote:

> In my opinion each individual substance always contains the marks of whatever has happened to it and the features of that which will ever happen to it ... Now every individual substance of this universe expresses in its concept the universe into which it has entered ... Now what is it to say that the predicate is in the subject if not that the concept of the predicate is in some manner involved in the concept of the subject? Since from the very fact that I began to exist it could be truly be said of me or that this would happen to me, we must grant that the predicates were principles involved in the subject or in the complete concept of me which constitutes the so-called ego and is the basis of the interconnection of all my different states. These have been known to God from all eternity.[3]

Leibniz did not use the words *exemplar* or *logoi*, but the principle he was discussing is remarkably similar. Since the ground of a thing's being is the Divine Mind, it follows that contained in the idea or form of that thing is all events that will occur in relation to that thing. God, being omniscient, is able to know all these infinite relations, but this brings to mind the logoi of Maximus Confessor, who argued that the logoi are the archetypes or forms of things that are also uncreated divine energies. Leibniz continued:

> This is a very important proposition that deserves to be well established, for it follows that every soul is as a world apart, independent of everything else but God; that is not only immortal and impenetrable but retains in its substance traces of everything that

happens to it ... That is to say, every substance
expresses the whole sequence of the universe in
accordance with its own viewpoint or relationship
to the rest, so that all are in perfect correspondence
with one another. [4]

These are fascinating speculations. For Leibniz, the definition of
a thing should include all the predicates included in the subject. This
is, so to speak, the divine vantage point, which has determined the
time and course of a thing's existence and thus knows all the infinite
relations of that thing to all other things. But Leibniz also seems to
hint at the idea of what would be discovered in DNA as he hinted
at the genetic history of a living thing's entire lineage.

Though we needn't accept Leibniz's idea of no physical interaction
between the monads, there is an element of the macrocosm/
microcosm doctrine here in that every monad contains within it
all the traces of the events of the rest of the universe. In other
words, we may have a correlation here with the modern discovery
that light encodes information. In fact, light can even be used to
transfer data, hearkening to the thesis of Dee I have mentioned:
"The smallest particle should be considered as a world full of an
infinity of creatures."[5] Leibniz again hinted at future discoveries of
biology and quantum physics, yet because we are not the Divine
Mind, we cannot infer all the infinite relations.

I judged, however, that we must not be indifferent
to the different grades of minds or reasonable souls,
the higher orders being incomparably more perfect
than those forms buried in matter, being like little
gods by contrast with the latter, and made in the
image of God, having in them some ray of the light
of Divinity. That is why God governs minds as a
Prince governs his subjects. [6]

Leibniz thought that God, being the Great monad, has governance of the minds of his subject monads, while the material and animal order are governed like machines. The light of divinity, however, does penetrate into the minds of the sentient beings under God's providence, so here we again see the doctrine of illumination.

He continued: "Every mind being a world apart, sufficient unto itself, independent of any other creature, containing the infinity, expressing the universe, is as enduring, as subsistent, and as absolute as the very universe of creatures."[7] Leibniz seems to picture these simple monads like the Great monad. They are miniature versions of God, the Great Simple Mind. But what is of particular note is the idea that, as the ground of reality, each monad expresses the universe in itself. The ray of divinity itself penetrates all these "divine sparks," giving them an *entelechy*, as Leibniz says, using Aristotle's term, or a primeval force.

He continued:

> Monads are the grounds not only of actions but also of resistances or passivities, and their passions reside in their confused perceptions. This also comprehends matter or the infinite numbers. I have always been very pleased, ever since my youth, with the morals of Plato and to some extent his metaphysics: also these two sciences go together as mathematics and physics.[8]

This is an unclear section, but he appears to say that the energies or forces of nature are ascribed by Leibniz, not to blind forces, but to divine monadic guidance.

Explaining further, Leibniz wrote:

> Furthermore every substance is like an entire world and like a mirror of God or indeed of the whole world which it portrays, each one in its own fashion;

almost as the same city is variously represented according to the various viewpoints from which it is regarded. Thus the universe is multiplied in some sort as many times as there are substances, and the glory of God is multiplied in the same way by as many wholly different representations of his works. It can indeed be said that every substance bears in some sort the character of His wisdom and omnipotence, and imitates him as much as it is able to; for it expresses, although confusedly, all that happens in the universe, past present and future, deriving thus a certain resemblance to an infinite perception or power of knowing. And since all other substances express their particular substance and accommodate themselves to it, we can say that it exerts its power upon all others according to the omnipotence of God.[9]

Leibniz saw the monads as mirrors that each reflect God, showing in a small part the infinite perfections of the Deity, each being stamped with the characteristic perfections of God through the ray of Divine Light that penetrates all things. But the next quote is the most interesting in terms of my thesis on these speculations and Dr. John Dee. Leibniz postulates in *The Monadology*:

It must be confessed, moreover, that perception and that which depends on it, are inexplicable by mechanical causes, which is by figures and motions. And, supposing that there were a machine so constructed as to think, feel and have perception, we could conceive of as enlarged and yet preserving the same proportions, so that we might enter into it as into a mill. And this granted, we should only find on visiting it, pieces which push one against another, but never anything by which to explain a perception. This must be sought for, therefore, in the simple substance and not in the composite or in the machine. Furthermore, nothing but this (namely perception and their changes) can be found in the simple substance. It is also in this alone that all the internal activities of simple substances can consist. The name of *entelechies* might be given to all simple substances or created monads, for they have within themselves a certain perfection; there is a certain sufficiency which makes them sources of internal activities, and so to speak, incorporeal automata.[10]

The monads seem to operate like an anima mundi for Leibniz but are created. However, they also seem to be able to contain information and function in an automated fashion. In the same section, a large artificial machine is posited as a possibility, yet Leibniz denies that it would be more than a machine. In other words, the functioning of a monad, as a self-contained data-storing automaton mirror of the rest of reality is directly linked to the idea of a large humanoid robot. Since reality contains a regular, uniform functionality and consistency, it would be *possible* to construct a replicant monad, yet it would not be a sentient being in the sense that humans and God are sentient. In other words, could monads be reverse engineered—could an artificial monadic machine be constructed that functioned automatically? In fact, it would appear so, since Leibniz is a key figure in the development of the logic machine we call the personal computer.

Consider Leibniz's process of inference, though. Because Leibniz accepted some basic Platonic presuppositions, he was able to deduce a host of inferences about metaphysics that, even if they aren't all correct, are correct enough to be the basic starting points for how to construct a unified machine that uses algorithms to replicate and store amazing amounts of data as well as accomplish a host of other activities.

Indeed, the amazing advance of artificial intelligence has a direct connection to the ideas of Leibniz and the Kabbalistic idea of the Golem since what Leibniz here describes is very close to the Golem theory. That theory would be possible only if certain metaphysical assumptions about the nature of reality and its uniformity were true. While the Augustinian identification of the mirrored archetypes in reality should not be identified with the divine essence, it is true that the Renaissance and Enlightenment notion of people's minds as mini mirrors of God was the basis for Leibniz's idea, yet he expanded it to encompass all reality—all reality is made up of infinite little rational mirrors. Light is ultimately derived from God in the first chapter of Genesis, and when it is combined with the theory of Dee, we can see the development of the idea that light encodes information. And, amazingly, this can be reproduced in the world artificially. Dee wrote in his *Monas Hieroglyphica* of the monad at length, adopting this Pythagorean and Platonic tradition with Leibniz:

Theorem XVIII

From our Theorems XII and XIII it may be inferred that celestial astronomy is the source and guide of the inferior astronomy. Before we raise our eyes to heaven, kabbalistically illuminated by the contemplation of these mysteries, we should perceive very exactly the construction of our monad as it is shown to us not only in the LIGHT, but also in life and nature, for it discloses explicitly, by its inner movement, the most secret mysteries of this physical analysis. We have contemplated the heavenly and divine functions of this celestial Messenger, and we now apply this co-ordination to the figure of the egg. It is well-known that all astrologers teach that the form of the orbit traversed by a planet is circular, and because the wise should understand by a hint, it is thus that we interpret it in the hieroglyph shown, which conforms in every detail with all that has gone before.[11]

For Dee, the monad is also an all-encompassing explanation of the mysteries of metaphysics. You'll notice as well that he includes the imagery of the egg, which comes from the ancient Greek mysteries as the form of the universe itself. Is it possible Leibniz saw an idea in his version of the monad that was similar to what Dee saw, and that led him to posit the idea of a machine that could operate in this fashion? Could a "magic mirror" machine be created that would, in an imitative sense, perceive and record data as well as transfer it through energy? Do we have, with the ideas of the ether and monads, the beginning of the idea of a logic machine that could mirror concepts like the human mind and mirror concepts through the light given to it by the divine rays that emanate from the Deity? Dee saw his monad as elucidated in life and nature, as did Leibniz. I think the same inasmuch as the computer itself functions in many ways like the monads of Leibniz and Dee. Indeed, Leibniz wrote about this in his *De Progressione Dyadica*. This page on the history of computers explains his formulation of binary computation:

> Though hard to believe, in his 3-pages treatise *De progressione Dyadica*, Leibniz even outlines a calculating machine which works via the binary system: a machine without wheels or cylinders— just using balls, holes, sticks and channels for the transport of the balls: "This [binary] calculus could be implemented by a machine. The following method would certainly be very easy to be implemented. [A machine with] holes, which can be opened and closed. They are to be open at those places that

correspond to a 1 and remain closed at those that correspond to a 0. Through the opened gates small cubes or marbles are to fall into channels, through the others nothing to fall. It [the gate array] is to be shifted from column to column as required for the multiplication. The channels should represent the columns, and no ball should be able to get from one channel to another except when the machine is put into motion. Then all the marbles run into the next channel, and whenever one falls into an open hole it is removed. Because it can be arranged that two always come out together, and otherwise they should not come out."[12]

Notes:

1 (pg. xli-xlii) Philip Weiner explained in my copy of Leibniz's works (*Leibniz Selections*):
2 Leibniz *First Principles: Foundations of the Sciences* (pg. 93)
3 . (pgs. 96-7)
4 (pg. 98)
5 (pg. 99)
6 (pgs. 108-9
7 (pg. 116).
8 (pg. 189)
9 (pgs. 301-2)
10 The Monadology (pg. 536)
11 *Monas Hieroglyphica*
12 ?

CHAPTER 10

Energetic Ether Metaphysics

Twentieth-century scholar of the history of Christianity Jaroslav Pellikan wrote in *Christianity and Classical Culture: The Metamorphosis of Natural Theology in the Christian Encounter with Hellenism*:

> "Everything that is in motion must be moved by something" [wrote Aristotle]. Gregory of Nazianzus, responding to Aristotle's identification of God as a "fifth element" alongside the traditional four *stoicheia*, asked: "What is the force that moves your fifth element [ether] and what is it that moves all things, and what moves that, and what is the force that moves that?"[1]

Modern science is very much interested in the question of quantum mechanics and yet it is still dominated by the reductionist, physico-biological model of reality. The spirit of dissection and quantification has resulted in numerous amazing discoveries surrounding the subatomic level of reality, which no one can deny. We learn that, at that an infinitesimal level, the interaction between mind and matter is highly nuanced and mysterious. The action of the observer appears to affect the result of the experimentation, especially in regard to examinations concerning light itself, which gives evidence of being both a particle and a wave. This dialectical, sneaky manifestation light produces suggests several things in my estimation that call into question the current reductionist models of reality, suggesting ideas much closer to older, ancient models in which fundamental metaphysics was based around principles like eidos, entelechy, *trópoi*, energeia, telos, and ether.

One of the central areas of research for quantum issues is CERN, the European Organization for Nuclear Research in Switzerland, and a central figure in nuclear research is, of course, Wolfgang Pauli. But I want to focus on Pauli with regard to philosophy, Platonism, theism, and metaphysics. In light of recent responses from atheists, it will be especially pertinent to consider the fact that the endeavor of quantum studies from the mind of Pauli and his inspirations were, in fact, based on Pauli's hermetic and Platonic presuppositions and speculations. I think that the electromagnetic forces in nature are unified by the very things that Pauli was looking into that pointed to older models of reality, especially ether. And when we consider that perception is an active, energetic presence that subtly interacts with its intentional objects, we are back at metaphysics, like Pauli.

Indeed, a survey of Eastern patristic metaphysics, sharing much with the Hellenic and Egyptian metaphysics that preceded it, demonstrates numerous insights into how we might construct different models that integrate and harmonize these disparate and seemingly unrelated sciences and topics. In the case of light, we have what appears to be a contradictory amount of evidence: is it a wave or a particle? In similar fashion, all reductionist models of reality end up placing particularity in the subject minds of humanity as something foisted upon the objective world with no way to bridge that gap. Since reality is monistic (all one type of thing), in the atheist/materialist view, we have with these sophists a return of the ancient atomists. (I am aware that atomists had a more sophisticated view than mere materialism.) Similarly, both Plato and Aristotle reduced all reality, at some level, to the One or monad, making temporal reality an emanationist iconographic manifestation of copies of that fundamental reality. For Plato it was the One; for Aristotle, it was *prima materia*. Modern scientific endeavor owes much of its heritage to Aristotle, of course, and in that respect, we should consider a fundamental error in Aristotle that remains today in all his monistic successors.

Aristotelian metaphysics is characterized by hylomorphism: the coming together of matter (*hyle*) and form (*morphé*) to constitute singular objects. For Aristotle, singular objects precluded the possibility of singular objects participating in the form of another. Dr. Philip Sherrard outlined the problem of hylomorphism with regard to its attempted use for Christian metaphysics. What will become evident is that the problem that arises in the Thomistic attempt at using it is the same problem found in modern, reductionistic physics.

In the position Sherrard lays out from the Platonic metaphysic, it is possible for a substance to constitute a unity with more than one substance present in it. The possibility of a real unity with really different multiplicities of substances involved in participation is not possible in the Aristotelian scheme, and the Eastern fathers of the first seven centuries involved the Platonic version of this issue, not the Aristotelian. This is how God is operant in the world in an immanent, energetic way, yet not diffused into it pantheistically. This is how they formulated a Christology of real theosis that did not dissolve humanity into the divine ousia.

Since humans, for Aristotle and Latin theologians, are composite creatures of body and soul, this duality in reference to hylomorphism creates a problem not just between God and the world, Christ and His assumed humanity, but also between any particular object and universals. If the intellect and soul are separate from the body, constituting its form, then it is difficult to see how it is possible for the soul to function separately. But for Aristotle, the form of man did not exist separately from the body, or from matter. The reason for this ultimately is that Aristotle's version of absolute simplicity was transferred from the ideal realm of Plato into the here and now.

For Plato, the One was ideal and perfect in another ideational realm. For Aristotle, universals were temporal. Both thinkers had obvious dialectics at work that were insurmountable given their respective systems. For Aristotle, the simplicity of substances was placed in the temporal realm resulting in the inability of a unity to retain its identity while participating in other forms. For Plato, the dualism was evident in the inability to bridge the gap from the realm of forms to our realm of flux.

In the modern world, the same problems are present in physics and the reductionist models of the universe. Monism and dualism are two sides of the same coin that ultimately converge upon one another. As has been posited many times, dialectics have determined the entire course of Western thought for millennia from the Greeks onward in time. In certain ways, the Egyptian metaphysic was better than its Hellenic progeny, yet even it and ancient Indian thought ultimately ended up in the same monism and/or dualism. Indeed, as Sherrard observed, the defining common denominator of perennial philosophies seems to be that ultimate reality is a wholly other, singular monadic/monistic super-essence of some kind. The existence and being of that super-essence are coterminous: potentiality and actuality synonymous in the absolute simplicity of the "super being."

Western dialectics has thus resulted in a host of insoluble dilemmas in philosophy, politics, and science, given the present models of metaphysics. It is here that I want to return to Pauli and his insights from archetypes and Platonism that exercised such a profound influence on his discoveries. We will see in these various articles and correspondences a connection between the inner and outer worlds, (psyche and physis), energies and consciousness (energeia and psyche), power and modality (entelechy and trópoi). In Dennis Slattery's paper, "Atom and Archetype: The Pauli/Jung Letters," he explains:

> Pauli suggests that the radioactive nucleus is an excellent symbol for the source of energy of the collective unconscious. It indicates that

consciousness does not grow out of any activity that is inherent to it; rather, it is constantly being produced by an energy that comes from the depths of the unconscious and thus has been depicted in the forms of rays from time immemorial.[2]

Pauli viewed the archetype of the atom as an image of the individual. The point in the monad, the atom, is therefore directly believed to have a correspondence to the singularity of the human consciousness, the self. The mode and functionality of the atom in terms of its energetic resonance shows a remarkably similar energetic movement that sends forth rays in the same fashion as does the mind of the individual.

In Alva Noë's famous book, *Action in Perception*, Noë picked up from the phenomenological tradition the idea of intentionality demonstrating the ever-active, or enactive thesis regarding perception. The subject is therefore always producing a symbiotic relationship of energetic interaction in interacting with the outer world. The data transmission, in other words, happens two ways. That the psyche sends forth rays of light itself also brings to mind ancient and medieval views of optics and perception from figures like Dr. John Dee. Since we know that light conveys information, this begins to make sense, as the "data flow" between the subject's psyche and the outer object is a two-way road. It is from this singular personal or hypostatic subject—the self—that we begin to see the model for all reality being personal, in reference to God. The embodied human subject is the microcosm of the incarnate divine Subject, the Logos.

I wrote in an earlier article on light:

> Fundamental to this spirit [ether] or substructure of all things is light. Light itself encodes information like DNA, and it is not by accident that modern theoretical physics is so entranced by zeroing in on the infinitesimally tiny particles that make

up energy. The actual nature or makeup of light remains a mystery precisely because the totality of reality and all events is itself encoded in light. It is also not by accident that all information we take into our eyes and process in our psyches is all done by the information encoded in light. This is also how light is now technologically able to transmit and encode data: it is simply mimicking the actual operation of light in nature. Indeed, much of what Darpa does is modeled on the natural world itself. ... [N]umbers do have a feel, because the universe is light, and is encoded information that are also archetypal geometrical forms, which include the intuitive, emotional "feel" a thing has.[3]

Slattery continued:

At this point Jung brings in explicitly the world of spirit, which has to this point in the conversation hovered along the margins. Now the duality of psyche-physics engages a third: the relation between matter—psyche—spirit. I want to quote Jung's own realization of psyche and matter as a response to Pauli's profound understanding of physics and psyche:

The psyche ... as a medium participates in both Spirit and Matter. I am convinced that it (the psyche) is partly of a material nature. The archetypes, for example, are Ideas (in the Platonic sense) on the one hand, and yet are directly connected with physiological processes on the other; and in cases of synchronicity they are arrangers of physical circumstances, so that they can also be regarded as a characteristic of Matter (as the feature which imbues it with meaning).[4]

You begin to see why I bring these seemingly disparate ideas together. Reality is very different from what is presented in mainstream academia, and when our models of reality drop the reductionist nonsense, amazing patterns and discoveries begin to emerge. Plato was wrong to disconnect the realm of forms from our world. Archetypal forms directly interact with the temporal realm through the ether, and the ether is itself a psychic, rational, energetic manifestation that includes actualities and potentialities that are not dialectically in tension. Concerning Werner Heisenberg, Wikipedia notes of Hylomorphism:

> The idea of *hylomorphism* can be said to have been reintroduced to the world when Werner Heisenberg invented his duplex world of quantum mechanics:
>
>> In the experiments about atomic events we have to do with things and facts, with phenomena that are just as real as any phenomena in daily life. But atoms and the elementary particles themselves are not as real; they form a world of potentialities or possibilities rather than one of things or facts ... The probability wave ... mean[s] tendency for something. It's a quantitative version of the old concept of *potentia* from Aristotle's philosophy. It introduces something standing in the middle between the idea of an event and the actual event, a strange kind of physical reality just in the middle between possibility and reality.[5]

Ether *is* this spirit, this energetic mediating realm of potentiality and actuality. It bridges the gap between psyche and world. Readers will see the similarity in Heisenberg's quote and the ideas of Jung and Pauli I have expressed. Quantum studies and the investigation of light is therefore intimately bound up in obvious metaphysical concepts! So much for Hume's jettisoning of metaphysics into the dustbin.

Readers will also recognize the connection to the mirrored aspect of reality—the correspondences (between atom and archetype)—I write about this on my website as well. When the monists and adherents of absolute divine simplicity collapse potentiality and actuality in God, they inevitably do the same for created reality as well, as I have illustrated with regard to Aristotle. If potentiality and actuality are synonymous in God, then by extension they become treated that way in nature, and thus there is no place for either. There is only ultimate potentiality (chaos) or ultimate (pure actuality, *actus purus*) static being. Being and becoming are therefore treated as another dialectical dilemma. Only if both are retained, as well as the middle term of ether, so to speak, is reality coherent. And that is precisely the kind of world we see demonstrated in the kind of energetic *ether* model I'm presenting.

Slattery continued:

> In the process of narrating a long dream sequence, Pauli concludes his description of a recurring image, whom he calls "The Dark Woman," by speculating that "there seems to be no essential difference between mirror symmetries in radioactive beta decay and multiple manifestations of an archetype" (p. 165)." The mirror symmetry of the correspondence between radioactive decay and the individual psyche's energetic interaction with the outer world is amazing. It is a mirror model of the same idea Noë was interested in, in *Action in Perception*. It is

a dualistic relationship that is only made coherent or rational by the third term, the energetic spirit that is manifested in the diagrams. The matter-mind, subject-object dualities are overcome because they are not in tension. They are harmonized by a third principle, the energetic *ether*, within which are actualities and potentialies. It is completely sensible if the universe is a microcosm of the macrocosm, with all the *logoi* summed up in the Logos. This means that atomic activity is also a microcosm of man himself as a macrocosm, as well as both being microcosms of the universe as macrocosm. In this way, the ground of reality is *psyche* and its *energeia*. Like Sherrard stated above, ether allows for interaction between these principles without either losing their identities. Matter and psyche are directly connected without losing what they are or being absorbed into the other.

God has imprinted on man's psyche a similar modality or *tropoi* as the outer world of "matter." Writers Atmanspacher and Primas comment on the Jung-Pauli letters with a particular insight:

The totality of the personality that entails both the conscious and the unconscious psyche is called the "self": an archetype representing the wholeness of man and, moreover, the goal of the process of his psychic development. This process is called individuation in Jung's parlance, and in his treatise Psychology and Alchemy, he unfolded the thesis "that there is in the psyche a process that seeks its own goal independently of external factors." [6]

Unless the self is an actually existing reality, science and its objectives are meaningless nonsense. Once topics like self and ether are discussed, metaphysics is back. The authors continued:

> Another example of an archetype which Jung considered to be particularly important was the principle of quaternity, reflected by structures like mandalas, squares, and crosses. According to Jung (1969b), "quaternity is an archetype of almost universal occurrence. It forms the logical basis for any whole judgment." Quaternarian structures—one could also say: structures based on the number four—can be interpreted as symbols of all concepts of unbroken wholeness, whatever they may be, in both psychology and in physics, in the internal and in the external world. The historical significance of quaternity in European culture can be traced back to the Pythagoreans where the tetraktys was the holiest of the numbers. It is implicitly used in various principles of systematic philosophy (cf. Kant's or Schopenhauer's fourfold classification schemes), and it is clearly seen in many distinctions of every day life: four points of the compass, four seasons, four basic colors, four dimensions of space-time, and so on. Jung's work on psychological functions suggests the four classes of thinking, feeling, sensation, and intuition. Individuation, i.e., the realization of the wholeness of one's self, is thus also meant as an integration of these functions. Quaternity often has a 3+1 structure, in which one of the four elements is of particular significance and creates "a totality" together with the other three. (An example: the dimension of time together with the three dimensions of space provides the

four-dimensional space-time structure of general relativity.) Jung's discussions with Pauli have often been about the principle of quaternity as compared to that of trinity, related to the number three. [7]

Amazingly, we are back at Pythagorean conceptions of the geometrical structure of reality that Pauli found appealing. As a theoretical physicist, Pauli was acutely aware of the importance of numbers and reality. Triadic and quaternion structures and archetypes are fascinating, mysterious manifestations. Pauli saw this and incorporated it into his postulation of the neutrino. For our purposes here, it is an example of the obvious patterns that bridge the gap between inner and outer worlds. As I wrote in my article "Numbers Prove God":

> The question of numerical entities was of peculiar interest to the ancient Greeks who, according to Plato's *Timaeus*, inherited their mystical and Pythagorean notions from Egyptian esoterism. It is also in the *Timaeus* that we are presented with an almost miraculous knowledge of the structure of miniscule reality (Platonic solids), seemingly impossible, given the technology of that time! Back to the argument—it occurred to me that in considering the transcendental argument for God, an overlooked, yet crucial component of this approach is the issue of numbers themselves. For those that are well-read in Maximus the Confessor and Philip Sherrard, an even deeper insight comes to the fore.[8]

Numeric patterns are immediately present everywhere and are involved in every act of predication, as I argued:

> Any time we predicate something of an object, we utilize principles and categories. This is unavoidable

and one of the things we assume is mathematical entities. All created reality can be categorized according to unity and difference. Thus, one and many are assumed in anything and everything. When I say, "That table," I am assuming a special unity of a specific object in my experience that is distinguished in that act by all other objects of perception. One is therefore assumed in any act of predication or communication. But "1" itself is not just a token symbol or sociological development, it is an actual objective principle, which is made evident by the fact that predication, communication and mathematics can be done across cultures and over time. If it were not invariant and objective, it would be subject to change like all material things.

"1" is not just 1. 1 is also infinitely divisible. Even Xeno was aware of the possibility that space could potentially be divided infinitely, and the result of this is that infinity is actually present at every point. When I say "point" here, I am referring to the Pythagorean and Platonic idea of the monad or point in geometric space and/or time. The 1 is therefore not merely 1, since it can be divided infinitely, it also encompasses an infinite potentiality within itself, as well as infinite potential relations to all other unities or objects. This is a peculiar problem for materialists especially, because for a materialist with the standard empiricist assumptions, the only "rational" thing to acknowledge is whatever can be (supposedly) retained from immediate sense experience. But even back to Berkeley's time, it was posited that infinity is surely a mathematical reality, yet no one has a direct sensuous experience of anything infinite.[9]

The one and many are reconciled here without any dialectical tension, but in symphonia. In order for this to make sense, the principle of telos must return to science and physics. Pauli was correct to critique Darwinism on this point.

In his article "Scientific and Epistemological Aspects of Concepts of the Unconscious," Pauli wrote:

> This model of evolution is an attempt to theoretically cling, according to the ideas of the second half of the 19th century, to the total elimination of any finality [telos]. As a consequence, this has in some way to be replaced by the introduction of chance. [10]

Pauli suggested that the concept of synchronicity might force science to revive the historically repressed concept of finality [telos] as a complement to causality. In "Die Vorlesung an die fremden Leute" (part of the very personal essay, "Die Klavierstunde"),[11] Pauli speculated about a "third kind of natural law which consists in correcting the fluctuations of chance by meaningful or functional coincidences of causally not connected events." But he hesitated to publish such thoughts: "If one really would like to make such ideas public, it would be imperative to show something which is verifiable."[12]

Pauli was no fundamentalist dummy; rather, he was a genius presenting the very thing we theists have argued for a long time: physics and metaphysics demonstrate a world like we present, not a meaningless, nonsense, chaotic world in which subjective minds impose random, relativist meanings on the external world. Instead, it is a vastly different cosmos in which the psyche and the outer world are joined by ether, and this ether is not some ridiculous idea, but an energetic luminous level of reality that undergirds and penetrates all else. It is the source of infinites, actualities, and potentialities, and it brings about telos. Interestingly, ether physics has returned to Oxford too. In a 2006 *New Scientist*, a paper was published that points in the direction of ether. It states:

Nineteenth-century physicists believed that just as sound waves move through air, light waves must move through an all-pervading physical substance, which they called luminiferous ("light-bearing") ether. However, the Michelson-Morley experiment failed to find any signs of ether, and 18 years after that, Einstein's special relativity argued that light propagates through a vacuum. The idea of ether was abandoned—but not discarded altogether, it seems.

Starkman and colleagues Tom Zlosnik and Pedro Ferreira of the University of Oxford are now reincarnating the ether in a new form to solve the puzzle of dark matter, the mysterious substance that was proposed to explain why galaxies seem to contain much more mass than can be accounted for by visible matter. They posit an ether that is a field, rather than a substance, and which pervades space-time. "If you removed everything else in the universe, the ether would still be there," says Zlosnik. This ether field isn't to do with light, but rather is something that boosts the gravitational pull of stars and galaxies, making them seem heavier, says Starkman. It does this by increasing the flexibility of space-time itself. "We usually imagine space-time as a rubber sheet that's warped by a massive object," says Starkman. "The ether makes that rubber sheet more bendable in parts, so matter can seem to have a much bigger gravitational effect than you would expect from its weight." The team's calculations show that this ether-induced gravity boost would explain the observed high velocities of stars in galaxies, currently attributed to the presence of dark matter.[13]

Jay Dyer

Indeed, this would make much more sense than the reductionist models. This would also point directly back to a unified field theory as well. As for my argumentation here, however, I think my speculative analysis should provide a good platform from which thinkers can springboard to other ideas that link ancient and Eastern metaphysics to recent discoveries. Of particular relevance is the needed reemergence of eidos, entelechy, trópoi, energeia, telos, and ether. We see these concepts emerge in thinkers like Leibniz, Dee, Newton, Pauli, proponents of unified field theory, and modern-day Platonist mathematicians and theoretical physicists. These theories and discoveries are amazingly in line with ideas founded in Eastern theology and ancient philosophy.

Notes:

1 Jaroslav Pelikan's *Christianity and Classical Culture,* pg. 66
2 (*Atom and Archetype*, p. 14)
3 ?
4 (pp. 100-01)
5 (*Quantum Reality: Beyond the New Physics,* pp. 26–27.)
6 (Jung, 1968, Ziff. 4).
7 ?
8 ?
9 ?
10 (Pauli, 1954a, p. 297)
11 Pauli, 1953c, Ziff. 41
12 (Pauli, 1953c, Ziff. 45)
13 2006 *New Scientist,* a paper

CHAPTER 11

St. Darwin's Space Brothers

We tend to think of science fiction, modern science (scientism), and religion as three distinct disciplines with minimal connection among them. When we consider them philosophically, however, a radically different perspective begins to take shape as the underlying presuppositions of all three converge. Considering the weaponization of culture under establishment rubrics of full-spectrum dominance, all three are crucial cultural drivers that disseminate a prepackaged worldview to consumers. Whether we consider Isaac Asimov fans, militant disciples of Richard Dawkins, or the followers of L. Ron Hubbard, all three groups have tremendous power to shape, mold, and convert the perspectives of their flocks toward a certain desired end. The end goal for this triad in our age of transition is an ultimate, singular, monoculture globo-worldview, one that will function as a kind of new religious mythology.

From the earliest days of what we know as science fiction, as conveyed by figures like Jules Verne and H. G. Wells, the notion of science as the means by which people may project their imaginations into the future was seen to be a useful tool of statecraft. Particularly with Wells we can see a figure whose stated goals of Fabian socialism would seep into many of his more notable works with beaming effulgence. Wells supposedly sought the eradication of the speculative monetary system (the close of *Outlines of History*), and through fantasy he foretold a bright era of technological utopianism in which reason would be crowned king. In books like *The Time Machine*, notions of eugenics play a central role in conditioning the coming eons for the rise of the control and management of the vulgar class by the technocratic control grid.

In stories such as *War of the Worlds*, the alien invasion myth exploded with even many of the academic class subscribing to the notion of civilizations that inhabited Mars or planets on other solar systems. Hollywood soon jumped on board, and after Orson Welles's famous broadcast, there would issue a nonstop flow of all things alien, UFO, and galactic as new luminaries like William Burroughs, Christopher Nolan, Robert Heinlein, Frank Herbert, Isaac Asimov, Arthur C. Clarke, and many more chipped in to produce classics in both print and screen incarnations. From the vantage point of propaganda, the state found the alien mythos to be quite a useful tool, piling on more and more external invasion "threats" as the fascinated masses consumed ever more. By the 1970s and '80s, following the ostensible *Apollo 11* mission, movies like *Close Encounters*, the Star Wars Trilogy, and *E.T. the Extra-Terrestrial* had crystallized the alien myth in the minds of the public as fact far more than scientists' claims of panspermia ever did.

It is precisely with panspermia that we see the infusion of the alien mythos into so-called empirical science accompanied by an absurdity made manifest by definition—no one has observed panspermia. It is simply a theory, and a sci-fi theory at that. Indeed, any film buff will tell you there is no foreseeable end to Hollywood's alien mythology.

Yet there's another "alien" story that is also crammed down our throats, which arises roughly contemporaneously with science fiction, and that is Darwinism. It is purported to be a strictly "natural" explanation of the "origins" of life and species adaptation (change over time), but the more we delve into the ideological origins of Darwinian theory, the clearer we see it to be linked with British Freemasonry and ancient mythology. Less and less does it appear to be "scientific," and more and more does it resemble another Wells tale. Having been redefined and elastically stretched to encompass everything from floor polish to toenails, literally all Creation is purported to be "proof" of evolution. Despite no transition fossils (and we should be swimming in endless piles of the billions of dead transition creaturely remains), Darwinism is the dominant vulgar religious perspective of our day with all reality coming under its aegis as a product of endless material flux and chaos.

Concurrent with this grand narrative explanation is the other tale of wonder—that offered by science fiction. Thus, while Darwinism looks to the past, science fiction is distinctly future oriented. Quite often the two meld together and are linked, especially in the alien mythos. The explanation for the "obviously rational" and "highly likely" existence of extraterrestrial entities in some form lies in the assumptions of Darwinism. Why, it's simply obvious that the solar system took 4.5 billion years to "form" (an unsubstantiated, non-empirical presupposition), so surely that would give rise to the birth of "life" on Zeta Reticuli—a star system almost forty light-years from Earth. And since we're speaking of billions of years, it's likely that those entities "evolved" to be far more advanced than us humans. Not only that, but they probably "seeded" us here on terra firma.

Pause for a moment. Doesn't that sound just like science fiction! However, let us recall our opponents' definition of science— observable "facts" to support or negate a theory. In other words, these are the creative speculations of humans in much the same way Bobba Fett and Mork are the products of Tinseltown fantasy. *They're not real!* Neither is the postulation that primordial muck was struck by lightning and gave birth to determined amoebas and fish and whales. Much as they do with science fiction, humans fashion for themselves surrogate myths. This is reminiscent of a child donning a Superman costume and leaping off the couch into the great beyond.

We see a window into this process of melding a new pseudo-religion in examples of UFO cults like the Raelians or "religions" like Scientology. Both purport to be in perfect harmony with science and critical of the present systems of petty government corruption—a contemporary echo of Wells's complaints in *Outlines of History*. Both project glorious futures of utopian progress through various pseudo-scientific and scientistic means, as man can achieve self-salvation through some rigorous process of bizarre doctrinal adherence. And both maintain a strict regimen of belief for followers—cult figures shall not be challenged since the cult has the monopoly on truth and the answers to pretty much any issue that might arise. And if they don't right away, have faith, for an answer will surely be delivered by the high priesthood. Sci-fi cults operate in the exact same fashion as the sci-fi cult of Darwinism in which dissent results in ostracism, unemployment, mockery, and harassment.

Despite the genocidal totalitarian regimes of the twentieth century basing their principles on Darwinism, reason, and science, resulting in the murder of millions, faith in the cult of the sci-fi Darwinian state of the future continues. You can buy microwaves and iPhones—and those are proof of evolution. Oh, you weren't aware? What are you, a slack-jawed Ozark Mountain dweller? You didn't know iPhones prove Darwinism? I can hear the *Deliverance* banjo theme playing right about now!

Of course, technological progress has absolutely no necessary connection to a wild biological theory of origins, but that never ceases to be submitted as a "proof" of a ridiculous model. One thing cult members lack is critical thinking and objectivity, and if the Darwinian science-fiction space opera that is to be our coming religion boasts anything, it's an army of followers who bloviate about reason while not possessing the foggiest idea that reason operates on immaterial, invariant principles that belong to the domain of metaphysics.

Once Darwin and the empiricists supposed they had banished metaphysics to the great nothingness, the past was assumed to be "explained" on "natural" grounds. But the future still needed hope, something for ever-deluded mass humanity to project into the stars (after all, we are all "stars" according to Krauss and Crowley), and the psy-op scions of science fiction deliver. To play with reality and rewrite it—as only a god could do—is the function of our new saints, St. Darwin and St. Wells, prophets and sages of the new dawn heralding humanity's extermination, as Holy Father Bertrand Russell lovingly prayed, with the aid of the space-brother elites intent on bringing us to childhood's end. It's just science.

CHAPTER 12

Darwinism and Creation

There are numerous misunderstandings surrounding the subjects of Genesis, Creation, evolution, science, and theology that muddy the primordial goo even further than it already has been. (If only it were real!) From reliance on naïve positivism and empiricism to assumptions and equivocations over terms, the standard debates on these issues are often ill served by both sides, including Creationists and/or intelligent design proponents, generally due to bad philosophy. The same is true for the opponents of Creation, who almost never have a background in the philosophy of science, which looks at the logos—the mechanics and workings—of the very thing they propose to practice and defend. The worst side of this matter is undoubtedly the Darwinian side, which I will argue is the most irrational and incoherent of all. Indeed, rather than a position that should be taken seriously and conciliated or reconciled to theology, it ought to be dispensed with as preposterous. My purpose is, in part, to respond to a recent defense of "theistic evolution" as well as to shed light on more fundamental, presuppositional problems in this often-misguided debate (with more to follow in the future).

The Evolution of Darwinian Evolution and Anti-Epistemological Self-Negation

The most misunderstood and simultaneously most important factor to grasp is the way presuppositions and paradigms function as templates to interpret "facts." An epistemological mistake that has become the entrenched norm since the Enlightenment's tabula rasa is the presumption that there are "brute facts" that come uninterpreted outside of some contextual framework or worldview. In the older paradigm, which retained a more classical anthropology in which humans were seen as created beings, humans were equipped with a host of faculties from God. They were endowed with the ability to will, act, learn, and modify their environment. This holistic view was grounded in a wide-ranging metaphysical anthropology inherited primarily from the Eastern Christian tradition and the Christology of the seven ecumenical councils, but also with terminological and conceptual insights and analogies from the Greek philosophical tradition.

The revolutions of the Enlightenment period repositioned humanity in a vast, mechanistic, determined cosmos of flux and brute "causality" in which people sought to become the ultimate agents and source of meaning itself. Western establishment science eventually came to reflect this revolution in thought by offering a new paradigm of the natural sciences in which humanity was now the chance product of endless eons of chaos and flux. The crucial point to keep in mind for our discussion is the fact that the purely "naturalistic" framework for understanding the world was promulgated with an astounding degree of propaganda and top-down dogmatism, notably from Britain's Royal Society (formerly The Royal Society of London for Improving Natural Knowledge). Evolutionary naturalism, as we will explore, is undoubtedly and certainly a conspiracy, and not at all a neutral theory of open scientific inquiry as it pretends to be.

It is this notion of scientific and epistemic neutrality that must be examined and dispensed with first. Presuming to interpret the phenomena of experience without a contextual framework or schema within one's lexicon of linguistic symbols becomes self-evident upon reflection, yet it mysteriously eluded so many of the empiricists of the last few centuries precisely because it contradicted their dogma of tabula rasa. Ironically, this is already an older, outdated philosophy of perception that perfectly mirrored the zeitgeist of Hume, Kant, and Locke. For those steeped in modern philosophy of science, phenomenology, and traditions counter to the Darwinian ethos, there are numerous indicators that show that the "facts" of our experience are rather parts of a network of signs and symbols. As well, they are situated within a "web" or our wider and more foundational beliefs and assumptions about the world.

The earthworm, for example, was famously hailed by Darwin himself, and still is by many of his disciples today, to be the most important "evolutionary appearance" prior to the supposed dawn of humanity. Let's take the earthworm as an example of how science actually functions on the ground, and let's consider what philosophical and perceptual truths emerge that, in fact, predate the actual praxis of the scientific method. The earthworm investigated in the lab is the earthworm as known, experienced, and interpreted by the individual scientist who works with the benefit of an inner framework of past experiences, accumulated knowledge, and present "direct" experiences with the slimy dirt dweller, all of which form an interpretation of the object before him in his lab. Upon reflection, it should be self-evident that the mechanics of how this creature is understood will be informed intuitively by the scientist's conceptions concerning it. In other words, the earthworm does not spontaneously generate its own, wholly new meaning to the fresh mind's eye; neither does a scientific blank slate of perception simply record quantitative "facts" about the object, add them all up, and produce an earthworm calculus for all such "species."

This earthworm did not appear out of a vacuum with an instruction manual; neither does the mere quantification of its length, weight, diet, and other habits afford the scientist all possible earthworm gnosis. While these points seem obvious to us as we read and ponder the actual actions of perceiving phenomena in any given scientific lab, this naïve empiricism is still the normative approach and presupposition for mainstream science! This, in fact, is why modern science tends to avoid the questions of philosophy of science, relegating them to the dustbin along with medieval metaphysics and angels because it pretends they are unanswerable. However, the questions are not unanswerable; rather, the answers to such questions and the explanations regarding them are not what mainstream science wants to hear.

It is obvious why this is so, as it immediately brings metaphysics back into the picture, but not only metaphysics; it immediately shows the inescapable need for, and usage of, invariant, immaterial, conceptual realities (such as laws of logic, mathematics, and other disciplines), which are not coherent in most paradigms of secular and naturalistic materialistic science. While I am not advocating Husserl's notion of "bracketing," he certainly showed, in his *Logical Investigations*, published at the turn of the twentieth century, that the scientific method operates on principles of logic, inference, coherence, and regularity that are *not* empirically knowable or verifiable,. For example, the principle of induction, upon which all of science is founded, cannot be known or verified empirically.

That the future will be like the past, as Hume consistently showed, cannot be known by past or present empirical observations without begging the question or being circular. In a Christian context, of course, we have a reason for believing the future will be like the past and nature will function with regularity. This is known as the Providence of God. While seemingly laughable and jeered at by modern self-negating people, this is perfectly coherent, if the kind of God professed exists, yet utterly incoherent in the worldview professed by the naturalist, and especially the naïve empiricist naturalist (which is the majority of that camp to this day). Indeed, that scientists are so ignorant of philosophy—and by extension logic—is really a folly to their own detriment and a source of most of this nonsense.

As philosopher of science Michael Polanyi commented:

> To say that the discovery of objective truth in science consists in the apprehension of a rationality which commands our respect and arouses our contemplative admiration, that such discovery, while using the experience of our senses as clues, transcends this experience by embracing the vision of a reality beyond the impression of our senses, a vision which speaks for itself in guiding us to an even deeper understanding of reality—such an account of scientific procedure would be generally shrugged aside as out-dated Platonism: a piece of mystery-(*Personal Knowledge*, p. 5–6) mongering unworthy of an enlightened age. Yet it is precisely on this conception of objectivity that I wish to insist in.[1]

But back to our scientist in the lab with his pet earthworm—from whence earthworm? Estimations (generally spouted as factual dogmas) of the earthworm's presumed genetic development will already be *assumed* to be what has been presented in the Darwinian paradigm. Similarities in genetic code with other worms will be *read* precisely according to the single ancestor thesis, proclaiming (with Darwin) this worm the "most influential" ancestor. The standard reply: "It came from a sea worm five hundred million years ago." Really? And how might this be determined, aside from so-called carbon dating? It is presumed from the hazy and monstrously speculative (and nonsensical) theory of the Darwinian "tree of life" of common ancestry.

So, from this example we can see the interpretation of the earthworm is bound up with its origins, already assumed to be the result of an arbitrary and preposterous claim of five hundred million years (!) based on a chart devised by an artistic rendering of a tree of life that was, in turn, *based on flawed semiotics*—the philosophy of interpreting signs and symbols—homologies and morphology—which literally amount to "Look how this thing looks like that thing—so there!" The example scientist in this case is relying on a theory that is based entirely upon authority, which he learned from his professors and other sources with no empirical means whatsoever for establishing anything approximating the fantastical dating of five hundred million years. The concept of half a billion years is so staggering and beyond human conception one wonders how supposedly learned men toss such figures around the same way they would recite the contents of last week's lunch.

Mystery Science Theater Time Lords from Planet X 5,000,000,000

A crucial few points should be added here concerning the "appearance of great age," which you will see in light of the earthworm. And my arguments that follow concerning phylogeny, morphology, and homology, are also subject to interpretation of appearances based on presuppositions. The only reason the layers of rock or calcite buildup are perceived to be ancient is that "experts," operating on all the same assumptions outlined here, proclaimed it to be so. It *must have* taken millions of years for geological formations to occur as they have. It simply *must have* taken millions of years for calcium carbonate to accumulate around geysers, stalactites, and stalagmites. The Grand Canyon *must have* developed over millions of years! Just look at it— you can see all those millions of eons in those layer-cake formations!

Yet, upon reflection, we realize there is absolutely nothing a priori that conveys any information whatsoever concerning vast eons of time when observing these structures. Quite the contrary—for every one of these common examples, there are observed examples of very brief spans of time in which similar structures have been observed to manifest! Ironically, there is *no* experiential, empirical basis for believing in the vast *eons* for dating these structures, given the very nature of the astounding and fantastical claims—60 *million* years, 4.5 *billion* years, and so forth. The Darwinian and naturalist modes of "science" are far closer to science fiction and H. G. Wells's vast eon propaganda than anything empirically observed.

Speaking of stalagmites, stalactites, and geysers, a geothermal geyser known as the Fly Ranch Geyser in Nevada is an accidental human Creation that resulted from drilling during exploration for geothermal energy. Over a few decades, this caused an exceptional pillar of calcium carbonate to form (along with two other similar structures). Mainstream science dates them up to 190,000 years even though it can be empirically and consistently proved that they formed in only *decades*. Similarly, identical phenomena can be seen in ancient caves and in basements of old houses that are only a hundred years old. Canyons similar to the Grand Canyon have opened up overnight; one example is the massive crack known as The Gash near the Bighorn Mountains in Wyoming in October of 2015. While not the same size as the Grand Canyon, it still is very large. The crack was the result of seismic shift, and it's formation proves that a larger Grand Canyon–sized hole could easily occur suddenly. It doesn't have to be the result of vast (unobserved) eons.

Polystrate fossils, which defy the eons of time, fit the same pattern of extending up through layers of substrate supposedly accruing over millions of years. Quite obviously, this is impossible on the mainstream model of dating (and rather clearly suggest a worldwide flood). The same principle applies for the purported idea that ice cores formed over eons. Also, objects have been found frozen in ice layers where they should not be according to traditional time lines. Astro/geophysics scientist Dr. Larry Vardiman agrees that the empirical pattern is consonant with short spans of time, not vast eons:

> The Greenland Society of Atlanta has recently attempted to excavate a 10-foot diameter shaft in the Greenland ice pack to remove two B-17 Flying Fortresses and six P-38 Lightning fighters trapped under an estimated 250 feet of ice for almost 50 years (Bloomberg, 1989). Aside from the fascination with salvaging several vintage aircraft for parts and movie rights, the fact that these aircraft were buried so deeply in such a short time focuses attention on the time scales used to estimate the chronologies of ice.

> If the aircraft were buried under about 250 feet of ice and snow in about 50 years, this means the ice sheet has been accumulating at an average rate of five feet per year. The Greenland ice sheet averages almost 4000 feet thick. If we were to assume the ice sheet has been accumulating at this rate since its beginning, it would take less than 1000 years for it to form and the recent-Creation model might seem to be vindicated.[2]

Setting aside the absurdity of the vast eons of time involved in this scheme, the point is clear concerning the understanding of the earthworm as an example for the interpretation of any scientific datum (as well as all phenomena of experience) inasmuch as no object of experience is independent of the totality of our familiarity of the object. Thus, the *philosophy of science* raises the question of how the naïve empiricism involved in the entirety of the concocting (not to mention undergirding) of this theory is at all tenable given what the view itself says about humanity. By this point, I mean that the kind of "human" proposed in this Darwinian scheme is not *created human*—not a person with a will, *psyche*, and *nous*; he or she is purely *natural man* or *woman*, which terms are merely nominalist expulsions of air from the lungs that signify some token object (and not signifying an actual metaphysical category). Darwinism is inescapably *anti-metaphysical* (we will come to theistic evolution in a moment) and devised precisely to be so. As St. Paul remarked, the "natural man cannot receive the things of the Spirit" (1 Corinthians 2:14).

The emergence of the Enlightenment tabula rasa was intended to enthrone humankind's reason and scientific enquiry as supreme while, within a few generations, humanity was dethroned in Darwin's scheme, relegating human reason to the logical consequence of also being a meaningless or nonexistent appearance of the same deterministic natural causes that produced humanity itself. Inexorably bound up in the determinist naturalistic fallacy, the "reason" and "consciousness" that purport to do science are negated and made meaningless by the naturalism and transformism that function as its "chosen" grand narrative. Just as free will, volition, and consciousness must be tossed aside, so also must reason and scientific knowledge go, as well as the self as additional metaphysical verbiage.

As I have remarked many times, these are all variations on the same argument concerning the impossibility of naturalistic materialism, given that its scientistic empiricism is self-refuting: the scientific method itself cannot be empirically known (neither can a host of other things, such as conceptual entities, numbers, logical laws, and so forth), and yet they obviously undergird and are used in the process of scientific enquiry. Physicalism is a dead-end absurdity, and the embracing of it makes people fools manifestly, especially when they pretend to possess the keys of all gnosis, simultaneously showing their foolishness in the very act of speaking, as their presuppositions negate their own self as a conscious being.

Subjective Semiotics Masquerading as Bare Empiricism and More Fraud

As for homologies, morphology, and phylogeny, it should be insightful for those who aren't aware that Ernst Haeckel was notoriously guilty of forging the very inception of this idea, and this is known to be so. Recall that homologies are the central basis for the entire theory as well as the so-called common ancestor "tree of life." (As we will see, DNA is not a basis for Darwinian theory at all—quite the contrary; it is one of the strongest refutations.) In 1996, *Creation* magazine published an article by Creationist Russell Grigg entitled "Ernst Haeckel: Evangelist for evolution and apostle of deceit." Grigg wrote:

> Haeckel's enthusiasm for the theory of evolution led him to fraudulently manufacture "evidence" to bolster his views. He was the first person to draw an evolutionary "family tree" for mankind. To fill the gap in this between inorganic non-living matter and the first signs of life, he invented a series of minute protoplasmic organisms which he called *Monera* (plural of *Moneron*). These, he said, were "not composed of any organs at all, but consist entirely of shapeless, simple homogeneous matter … nothing more than a shapeless, mobile, little lump of mucus or slime, consisting of albuminous combination of carbon."[3]

In 1868, a prestigious German scientific journal published seventy-three pages of his speculations, with more than thirty drawings of these imaginary *Monera,* as well as scientific names such as *Protamoeba primitivia,* and the process of fission by which they allegedly reproduced, even though his detailed descriptions and elaborate drawings were totally fictional, as these "life particles" were entirely non-existent.

Later the same year, Thomas Huxley, Darwin's champion in England, reported finding something that fitted Haeckel's descriptions in mud samples that had been dredged from the bottom of the north Atlantic and preserved in alcohol. Huxley named them *Bathybius haeckelii*.

Haeckel is also famous for his faked sketches of supposed embryo similarity titled the "biogenetic law" of phylogeny. Grigg again:

> In his book *Natürliche Schöpfungs-geschichte* (*The Natural History of Creation*), published in German in 1868 (and in English in 1876 with the title *The History of Creation*), Haeckel used the drawing of a 25-day-old dog embryo which had been published by T.L.W. Bischoff in 1845, and that of a 4-week-old human embryo published by A. Ecker in 1851–59. Wilhelm His, Sr (1831–1904), a famous comparative embryologist of the day and professor of anatomy at the University of Leipzig, uncovered the fraud.
>
> Prof. Wilhelm His showed in 1874 that Haeckel had added 3.5 mm to the head of Bischoff's dog embryo, taken 2 mm off the head of Ecker's human embryo, doubled the length of the human posterior, and substantially altered the details of the human eye. He sarcastically pointed out that Haeckel taught in Jena, home of the then finest optical equipment available, and so had no excuse for inaccuracy. He concluded that anyone who engaged in such blatant fraud had forfeited all respect and that Haeckel had eliminated himself from the ranks of scientific research workers of any stature.[4]

This fraud has also been reexamined to be far more profound than many assumed. What the embryonic homology example and the Berkeley website's examples show is that this theory is fundamentally about recognizing patterns, which is an interpretation of forms, assuming all manner of conclusions based on unsubstantiated starting points. This is semiotics—interpreting forms and symbols, a very philosophical and subjective enterprise, though this is never admitted by those who proffer this scheme's simple, observable "empirical proof." Furthermore, this is not mere pattern recognition, which might be objective were it concerning mathematical samples, but instead, the various patterns involved in homology and morphology are not readily apparent. This subjective element to the phylogeny of Darwinism is laughably revealed when the Understanding Evolution website includes the following "probably" caveat, with the ridiculous, arbitrary conclusion "birds are dinosaurs" (italic emphasis mine):

> The process of evolution produces *a pattern* of relationships between species. As lineages evolve and split and modifications are inherited, their evolutionary paths diverge. This produces a *branching pattern* of evolutionary relationships ...

> The tree is supported by many lines of evidence, but it is *probably not flawless.* Scientists constantly reevaluate hypotheses and compare them to new evidence. As scientists gather even more data, they may revise these particular hypotheses, rearranging some of the branches on the tree. For example, evidence discovered in the last 50 years suggests that birds are dinosaurs, which required adjustment to several "vertebrate twigs."[5]

Quite a required adjustment to say the least! The entirety of this nonsense is based on the *assumption* of a common ancestor (never

141

demonstrated, only assumed—how could you possibly demonstrate this?), which is alternately defended on the claim of "similar DNA" and variations on that claim, such as endogenous retroviruses (ERVs). However, the small percentage of DNA differentiation between human and mouse, for example, obviously reveals a vast disparity in features, making the oft-cited monkey similarity example useless and absurd. Yet that is the point; we are told that the common DNA *must have* originated in a common ancestor, which is assumed to be the only rational thesis, as if God could not have created separate forms or species simultaneously. However, in a Creation paradigm, it makes perfect sense why common DNA exists—the same Designer created and coded all species from the same material of sea and earth (Genesis 1:11, 20, 24; 2:7). This is even taught visually in the icon of Creation by the logos.

The cry here will inevitably be that no supernatural causes can be invoked when doing "science." Such claims aren't scientific; however, the nature of the argument is precisely about divine origins, making this arbitrary setting of the parameters of the debate to exclude the matter under examination (God) from the outset! A purely natural explanation of origins works only if it's true, and that is what is being considered. Since both paradigms—naturalism and Christian theism—ultimately rely on assumptions that cannot be justified and are thus self-referential, the only resort is to look at internal coherence for each paradigm. Which paradigm can make sense of the process of science itself as well as how science—and ultimately knowledge itself—is even possible? This is a transcendental argument. Since the scientific method cannot be demonstrated empirically or known through the scientific method (circularity), both paradigms rest on a form of self-referentiality as shown, for example, in Kurt Gödel's incompleteness theorems. This is in contrast to the classical foundationalist epistemology of followers of the Enlightenment and earlier Western thinkers. The Christian theist falls back on the Christian system of belief and revelation as a governing paradigm, including understanding the natural world, while the naturalist relies on radical human epistemic autonomy, which is ironically negated in a general denial of consciousness and free will. With this framework analysis in place, I hope my approach will be made clear. It is in this manner that we must examine the Darwinian paradigm and set it against the Christian view to see which presentations make it possible to even do science, and which negates that possibility. Once the Darwinian paradigm is understood for what it actually is—*pseudoscience* masquerading as the preeminent catch-all grand narrative pinnacle of gnosis—it will become clear how it is not only impossible to reconcile with Creation and the origin of humanity. It will be seen as so incoherent and contradictory as to make its adherents moronic: "The fool has said in his heart there is no God" (Psalm 14:1). A scientific theory ought to be coherent and consistent on its own grounds before we choose to adopt it, and before we kowtow to the establishment's desire to reconcile it with theism in some form, we ought first examine its fundamental premises to see how bankrupt and preposterous it truly is. I can only think that the desire for accolades and the fear of being ostracized are generally the sources for such a desire to wed theism with this retarded cousin, but the offspring of such a pairing will sadly result in an exceedingly unfit mongoloid mutation.

Creation as a Revealed Doctrine and Thomistic Compromise

"Through faith we understand that the worlds were framed by the word of God, so that things which are seen were not made of things which do appear" (Hebrews 11:3).

Contrary to Thomism for example, Creation ex nihilo is not a doctrine that is proven through purely rational enquiry to autonomous humanity; neither is it perceived directly upon investigation of the external world. While there are many factors that may contribute evidence toward Creation, and certainly were humanity to perceive the world aright, Creation is the only rational position possible. While that is technically true, for Thomism, the natural world testifies to only a generic "first cause," purported to be of some different, more supreme substance than the created order. This flawed method of argumentation, based as it is upon a faulty Thomistic anthropology devoid of the nous, undergirds most classical apologetics. God as argued for by an Aquinas or an Etienne Gilson is described as a Being for whom the declaration of Exodus 3:14 signifies "I AM Being."

This Greek philosophical exegesis of the biblical text is certainly not what Moses or the Spirit of God had in mind when the text was recorded, and quite contrary to these speculations, the declaration is at once personal. This is why the so-called classical apologetics function to prove any sort of generic theistic first cause. Perhaps that first cause is a multitude of gods; perhaps it's the Islamic deity, perhaps the Mormon one. This "being" is not the God described in the biblical text, Who considers His existence *certain*, as do His followers (Acts 2:36), despite Aquinas's and others' contention God cannot be certainly known to exist—only with a *high degree* of probability. This is because, for Thomism, science is a matter of empirical experience and natural reason, while faith is a matter of supernatural grace.

For example, Aquinas explained his principles in seminal sections of the *Summa Theologica*, demonstrating his "classical foundationalist" (roughly empirical) epistemology synonymous with his two-tiered nature and grace assumption, as well as how this approach is conditioned from the outset by his rejection of the nous and belief in the Beatific Vision: God *cannot be seen directly and empirically in this life*, contrary to the Eastern dogma (emphasis mine):

> On the contrary, No one can mentally admit the opposite of what is self-evident; as the Philosopher (Metaph. iv, lect. vi) states concerning the first

principles of demonstration. But the opposite of the proposition "God is" can be mentally admitted: "The fool said in his heart, There is no God" (Psalm 52:1). Therefore, *that God exists is not self-evident.*

Reply to Objection 1. The existence of God and other like truths about God, which *can be known by natural reason, are not articles of faith,* but are preambles to the articles; for *faith presupposes natural knowledge,* even as grace presupposes nature, and perfection supposes something that can be perfected. Nevertheless, there is nothing to prevent a man, who cannot grasp a proof, accepting, as a matter of faith, something which in itself is capable of being scientifically known and demonstrated.[6]

Aquinas continued (emphasis mine): "I answer that, All science is derived from self-evident and therefore *'seen' principles*; wherefore *all objects of science must needs be, in a fashion, seen.*"

Now as I stated above (Article 4), it is impossible that one and the same thing should be believed and seen by the same person. Hence it is equally impossible for one and the same thing to be an object of science and of belief for the same person. It may happen, however, that a thing that is an object of vision or science for one is believed by another, since we hope to see some day what we now believe about the Trinity, according to 1 Corinthians 13:12: "We see now through a glass in a dark manner; but then face to face." *The angels possess this vision already,* so what we believe, they see. On like manner, it may happen that what is an object of vision or scientific knowledge for one person, even in the state of a wayfarer, is, for another person, an object of faith because he or she does not know it by demonstration.

Nevertheless, that which is proposed to be believed equally by all is equally unknown by all as an object of science: such are the things which are of faith simply. *Consequently faith and science are not about the same things.*

Faith and science are not about the same things because, for Aquinas, the logoi are not immanent in Creation through the divine energies of the logos. Aquinas was also explicit in his rejection of the divine energies, citing and rejecting St. John of Damascus on the very point, affirming absolute divine simplicity and affirming that God's actions and existence are His essence in strict identification. This point is stressed so many times in the *Summa Theologiae* that it is absurd to have to constantly debate it. For one example, Thomas says:

> Article 2. Whether any name can be applied to God substantially?
>
> Objection 1. It seems that no name can be applied to God substantially. For Damascene says (De Fide Orth. i, 9): "Everything said of God signifies not His substance, but *rather shows forth what He is not; or expresses some relation, or something following from His nature* or *operation [energy]*."
>
> On the contrary, Augustine says (De Trin. vi): "The being of God is the being strong, or the being wise, or whatever else we may say of that *simplicity whereby His substance is signified.*" Therefore all names of this kind *signify the divine substance.*
>
> Therefore we must hold a different doctrine—viz. that these names *signify the divine substance,* and are predicated substantially of God, although they fall short of a full representation of Him. Which is proved thus. For these names express God, so far as our intellects know Him. Now since our intellect

knows God from creatures, it knows Him as far as creatures represent Him.[7]

Now, why, in the midst of this discussion of Darwin and evolution, would I bring Thomism into the picture and pull out these dense theological issues? Somewhat near this period of Aquinas, the fourteenth-century East was debating these very underlying points with the West, as embodied in the discussion between Barlaam the Calabrian and St. Gregory Palamas. The debate was a manifestation of an Augustinian with an Orthodox, resulting in the affirmation on the part of the East of Palamism, which is incorrectly titled, as it is the classical Orthodox view, and in that debate Palamas specifically predicted that the Western trek would be to banish God from the created order through banishing His immanent energies. As a result, only the created effects of God are known, leaving Palamas to title the entire project atheism. Indeed, it is the Thomistic approach and its presuppositions that *unwittingly* led to the purely naturalistic empiricism that would reach its apogee in the West in Darwin. I have detailed this at more length in this piece. Fr. John Peck, a Russian Orthodox priest and pastor of an Orthodox church in Arizona, commented:

> In his 150 Chapters St. Gregory demonstrates that the failure to distinguish between the essence and energies in God leads either to atheism or polytheism. He argues that if the energies of God are created then they of necessity belong to a created nature, for as St. John Damascene writes, the energy distinct from the divine substance is a natural one. St. Cyril writes that Creation belongs to the divine energy, and so if the energy in God is itself created, then we must seek out an uncreated energy behind it which gave rise to it. If there is but substance in God, then there is no Creation, operation, or

relation to be found, which means He is not the principle and Lord of the universe, and destroys the trihypostatic Godhead, "And one who is not trihypostatic nor master of the universe is not even God. Therefore, those who thus hold the opinions of Barlaam and Akindynos are atheists."[8]

Theistic Evolution: A Doomed Marriage Officiated by Jesuits

It is from this ethos that the modern scientistic rationalism arose, coming as it did from the division Aquinas laid down as I've quoted here, despite his own intentions. The logic is obvious: The natural world can be known and understood without reference to revelation in large part as an aspect of "natural reason" apart from the logos. Hopefully, Thomas goaded, please would please possibly tack Jesus and the Trinity and Mother Church onto the science at some point down the road because they're sure-fire helpers! On the contrary (to use Thomas-speak), the Logos is the beginning, middle, and telos of all Creation and all human cognition, He being apprehended directly by the nous, not by intellect and psyche passing judgment on His existence upon supposed accumulations of empirical evidences. Intellect and psyche serve the nous, not the reverse, and the nous is the faculty for perceiving God directly in Creation through His incarnation, in which all of Creation is recapitulated into the Logos who created it to begin with: "And he is before all things, and by him all things consist" (Colossians 1:17). Also, we read in Hebrews 11:3: "Through faith we understand that the worlds were framed by the word of God, so that things which are seen were not made of things which do appear." That is true whether it is acknowledged by the unbeliever or not.

With the West's acceptance of these presuppositions (Thomism is still the official philosophy of the Roman Church), the dominance of naturalism was only a matter of time; it logically follows that the "scientific method" would toss away the "first cause god" who *cannot be seen in nature.* Aside from created analogical effects, this god eventually functioned as a useless placeholder atop a chain of generic being. If empirical knowledge is the assumption, and empirical knowledge never attains to this deity (in this life), what use of what certainty or reason do we have to think it exists? What relevance does a Supreme Substance have to the life of everyday Catholics? Of course, the rank and file weren't concerned with a supremely simple philosophical substance, but with the *personal* God they heard about in the liturgy in narrative form. Nevertheless, the academic and churchly establishment of the West marched on, *Summa Theologiae* in hand, handing over their heritage inch by inch as the centuries passed, fulfilling the prophetic words of St. Gregory Palamas. The end result would be atheism.

With that in mind, it becomes clear why the Roman Catholic Church also gradually adopted the German higher critical methodologies of revisionist excising of all the texts, eventually New Testament and Old until, at the hands of liberal Jesuits and "scholars," the entire Bible was ripped into nothing. Ironically, even the sainted Roman Pope Pius X explicitly and with full papal authority (for their communion) rejected higher critical methods and modernism as heresy across the board and unequivocally. (See "Lamentabili sane," "The Syllabus of Errors," 1907.)

Why is all this relevant? Because the same specious and fantastical presuppositions of Darwinian theory are the presuppositions of the unbelieving academics who fostered higher criticism as a conspiracy, grounded on a documentary hypothesis known as the JEPD Theory of the Torah, which upholds the tradition that the Pentateuch was written by Moses, an idea that many secular biblical scholars no longer adhere to in our day! Indeed, the Darwinian metaphysical assumption of all things being subjected to constant flux—if that is true—must also apply to religious doctrines, texts, and traditions, making the confessions of various religious bodies subject to the ebb and flow of the great God flux. Ironically, the father of higher criticism, nineteenth/twentieth-century biblical scholar Julius Wellhausen, admitted that his documentary approach was part of his own personal agenda—he *hated* the Mosaic texts.

Thomism's assumption of rational, autonomous humanity judging God to be existing or not based on "evidence" is come to full fruition in rational people judging the texts to be erroneous, exaggerated, superstitious, and mere mythologies. And we all know many of the later pioneers of evolutionary theory were Jesuits who, although not ardent followers of Thomas, were and are ardent believers in the assumptions of classical foundationalist epistemology. For example, in Archbishop Fulton Sheen's "defense" of the biblical texts, he adjures readers to make up their own minds with regard to "inspiration" based on the available "evidence." (For further information, consult chapter one of his book, *The Life of Christ*.)

Given the Roman Communion's belief since Cardinal Newman and Vatican I in the evolution and tree-like growth of dogma in the late nineteenth century (How else can Vatican I be made sense of?), it's only natural that the communion as a whole would become an ardent evangelist for Theistic evolution, which finally gives way to the wild absurdities, process philosophy, and occultic-flavored gobbledygook of rabid evolutionists, such as Teilhard de Chardin (a man once excommunicated, then "rehabilitated" after Vatican II in the 1960s, whatever that means). Teilhard, you will recall, was also involved in one of the more notorious frauds of Darwinian invention—the infamous faked Piltdown Man, fossil of England's so-called most ancient human ancestor—as even American paleontologist and evolutionary biologist Stephen J. Gould argued. By the way, the Darwinians speak of reading patterns—are you beginning to see a pattern concerning the frauds in this entire atheistic enterprise? (An excellent critique of Teilhard de Chardin by Dr. Philip Sherrard can be found on the Wayback Machine website: https://web.archive.org/web/20170507160049/http://www.studiesincomparativereligion.

com/public/articles/Teilhard_De_Chardin_and_the_Christian_
Vision-by_Philip_Sherrard.aspx.)

No New Codes in the Fly Soup

It is my contention that the presence of believing persons among
the ranks of Darwin believers is absolutely and utterly irrelevant.
So what if twentieth-century Ukrainian-American geneticist and
evolutionary biologist Theodore Dobzhansky and Archbishop
Greekopoulous and the Patriarch of Constantinople, along with
the popes to boot, all believe in Theistic evolution? None of those
persons amounts to anything in contrast to almost the entire history
and tradition of the Church, East and West, in contrast to a recent
Orthodox writer defending Theistic evolution. Everyone knows there
are countless heretical patriarchs and bishops, and what evangelicals
do or do not hold to six-day Creation is *also irrelevant*. Protestant
fundamentalists hold to the virgin birth—is that also a doctrine
of Western dialectical Creation? Of course not, and neither is the
revealed doctrine of Creation. Dobzhansky, it must be understood,
was a student of the Western Darwinian milieu, adopting the
guiding presuppositions of his masters, like Royal Society illuminist
Julian Huxley, in proclaiming "Nothing In Biology Makes Sense
Except in the Light of Evolution," Dobzhansky's essay that echoes
the Gospel of arch-villains the Huxleys: "Medieval theology urged
men to think of human life in the light of eternity—*sub specie
aeternitatis*: I am attempting to rethink it *sub specie evolutionis*—in
the light of evolution."[9]

Dobzhansky's famed fruit fly research proved that different
populations of the same species did not have identical sets of genes.
The irony of this experiment is that it in no way demonstrates or
proves transformism—that *new species* arise from environmental
pressures. Setting aside the fact that in the Darwinian ethos
the notion of a species is never clear or coherent, the mutations

purported to be observed in the lab presuppose the rise of a new species at some future date. Ironically, the DNA information in any species is never new information; it is only the switching on or off of existing information in that species. The earthworm, at no point and in no case or example, will never produce whale DNA. A bear that is fond of swimming over its several-decade lifetime does not begin to produce *new* duck DNA, as if webbed feet might appear. This admitted fact of DNA across the board is one of the strongest evidential arguments against the thesis of Darwinism, given that its theory of transformism necessitates *new information in the code.* This is why junk DNA, a much propagandized catch-all "proof" of evolution, has now been discarded. Even Richard Dawkins dishonestly altered his views, claiming he never did (though he's on video contradicting himself). Furthermore, Dobzhansky was a Teilhardist who rejected a personal God, Providence, and many other dogmas, stating, "Natural selection is a blind and a creative process. It does not work according to a foreordained plan."[10]

In conclusion, the fear and desire for compromise with this theory is really the result of misunderstanding the position's actual claims, as well as numerous equivocations about terms such as *adaptation.* Until the presuppositions of this paradigm are examined and challenged, the evidence will always be stretched or cut to fit the facts, as demonstrated in Thomas Kuhn's famous book, *The Structures of Scientific Revolutions.* Only when this and the countless instances of reliance on the fallacy of consensus and authority are properly understood will Darwinian naturalism truly be unmasked as nonsensical, irrational, contradictory, and intellectually bankrupt. Only when the countless instances of fraud and dishonesty are understood will it be seen to be an empty, destructive thesis. Evolutionary theory is not scientific; it is an enforced religious mythology from the halls of the Masonic Lodge, not an honest theory from the labs of academia. It is a position grounded on atheistic presuppositions at war with revelation and theism despite its popularity amongst theists. Not only is the theory a sure path to apostasy; it is a silly way to go. A biblical theist *should be scientific*, and that is why I could never adopt Darwinism or its mutation, theistic evolution.

The other consistent dishonesty on this topic is the claim that adaptations, which no one denies, are equivalent to new species. They are not. An adaptation is an alteration in the *existing* information, and never a foreign code and *never* the empirical observation of a new species! The assumption is that the mutation must be the source for the rise of a new species over vast eons of time because of the assumption of common ancestry! At once the circularity becomes apparent in this theory, as the proof of transformism is based on the unfounded assumption of common ancestry, while common ancestry is in turn based on the assumption of new species arising from long periods during which multiple mutations occurred. Neither of these ridiculous and sophistical positions is ever observed, and all are predicated on an interpretive matrix foisted on the "evidences" such as bones, fossils, and DNA.

At this juncture, I will mention that certain fathers like Augustine held to some speculative view of the first chapter of Genesis. And certainly other fathers in the East held to different opinions on the serpent, the meaning of this day and that, and so on, but that is not our purpose here. This matter has been dealt with extensively by many writers such as twentieth-century American Russian Orthodox hieromonk Fr. Seraphim Rose in his excellent book, *Genesis, Creation, and Early Man*, but it is also sufficient to say the traditional presentation of St. Basil the Great's nine homilies known as *Hexaemeron* is normative for the Orthodoxy of that period, and the majority of the Church. If you have not read it, I recommend you do so, especially before attempting to meld your faith with the absurdity known as Darwinism. Another misunderstanding to keep in mind is that, whatever patristic opinions might have been had on certain texts in the first three chapters of Genesis, *none* of those is coherent, compatible with, or suggestive of the Darwinian thesis (not even Augustine's view). The patristic consensus in no way allows for humanity to arise on the scene after the emergence of death, a preposterous and heretical opinion in Orthodoxy, yet necessitated by Darwinian eons. Death—all death, spiritual and physical—is explicitly the result of humanity's fall, as steward and covenant head of Creation. This is why the Logos recapitulates all Creation in His Incarnation as the New Adam and covenant Head (Colossians 1:15).

Conclusion

As an addendum, I recommend the excellent interview with American author Dr. David Berlinksi that highlights of the major flaws in this ridiculous position from a secular vantagepoint that make it utterly unappealing. Once people really understand this position, it escapes me why anyone would want to adopt this view, much less combine it with theism.

Notes:

1   (*Personal Knowledge*, p. 5-6)
2   ?
3   ?
4   ?
5   ?
6   ?
7   ?
8   [Chapter 134, p. 241]
9   See Lamentabili sane, The Syllabus of Errors, 1907
10 ?

● **CHAPTER 13** ●

Cryptography of the Cryptocracy

In January of 2014, International Monetary Fund (IMF) Chief Christine Lagarde gave a speech that was lost on most of her audience and amongst the media. She stated:

> Now, I'm going to test your numerology skills by asking you to think about the magic seven, okay? Most of you will know that seven is quite a number in all sorts of themes, religions. And I'm sure that you can compress numbers as well. So if we think about 2014, all right, I'm just giving you 2014, you drop the zero, 14, two times 7. Okay, that's just by way of example, and we're going to carry on. So 2014 will be a milestone and hopefully a magic year in many respects. It will mark the hundredth anniversary of the First World War back in 1914. It will note the 70th anniversary, drop the zero, seven— of the Bretton Woods conference that actually gave birth to the IMF.[1]

In his classic *Secret Societies and Psychological Warfare*, Michael Hoffman wrote of coincidence, synchronicity, and curious connections between 007 and 2001 that also relate to obscure subjects like numerology and gematria. The first 007 was Dr. John Dee, as will be investigated here, but the reason this is of import is the similarity between Christine Lagarde's seemingly strange comments to her Press Club audience. Hoffman has recently commented on this, and I myself, at the time of Lagarde's comment, speculated on the connections between the numbers of sevens that appeared in the downed Malaysian plane incident(s). Numerous conspiracy websites and speculators got in on the action, but what no one (other than Hoffman) did was look at the motivations behind such a mindset. The natural approach of those in conspiratorial and alternative media circles would be to leap at the occult. While I don't intend to deny such associations, I would like to highlight another element that almost none have considered. Yes, there are believers in dark forces in high places, but there is also another factor that should be kept in mind, as I myself had conversations with individuals about this that appeared a frightened by such calculating mumbo jumbo.

Simon Singh, in his recent book, *The Code Book*, explains of the process of cracking ciphers and codes as follows:

> Kerchoff's Principle: The security of a crypto-system must not depend on keeping secret the crypto-algorithm. The security depends only on keeping secret the key. In addition to keeping the key secret, a secure cipher system must also have a wide range of potential keys. [2]

As researchers and analysts of the world historical, we attempt to do just this on a much grander scale. Discovering the secrets of nature and supernature yields fulfilling mental rewards in their own right, but they also free us from the slavery to superstition. While I have attacked the Enlightenment many times over, and I think I am right in doing so for its excesses, it's also worth considering the positive aspects of the Enlightenment because it did serve to rid the Roman-dominated West of numerous bizarre superstitions and excesses that should not be excused. I doubt many of us in modernity would truly like to return to a world in which we expect to almost certainly be damned, spending our days working out a complex system of penitential indulgences to try to settle debts in an absurd punishment-based system. Such is part of my reason for leaving Western Christianity years ago, but this should also not be seen as endorsement of one side of a false Western dialectic of Rome versus Enlightenment. On the contrary, the truth lies somewhere in between extremes that the cunning of history is yet to work out (as we still live under the excesses of the quantification-obsessed Enlightenment). Let us see if we can locate at least one key for cracking the code of our modern overlords and decipher the Lagardian linguistic mysteries, surveying numerology, biblical gematria, and cryptography.

First, the subjects of numbers, numerology, and ancient perspectives on them, are helpful. For ancient man, numbers were magical, semi-divine entities that somehow related to all things, despite being in no particular time and locale. Obviously, in a book such as this, the scope of such an analysis must be limited, so I have chosen influential representative examples. My friend James Kelley explains in his "Prajapati Purusa and Vedic Altar Construction" essay the means by which the Pythagorean theorem was actually encoded in Vedic altar designs much earlier than the time of Pythagoras himself:

> This blurb fails to mention the amazing insights of Dr. Abraham Seidenberg, who found the so-called "Pythagorean theorem" at work in the Indian texts known as the *Sulvasūtras*, which date from the 8th century B.C., but which crystallize procedures and teachings that reach back into the Neolithic mists. Though historians of mathematics before Seidenberg noted the connection between the famous theorem and Vedic texts, it is our contention that Dr. Seidenberg was the first to offer a coherent

presentation of the *significance* of this influence. The *Sulvasūtras* contain explicit instructions for how to construct the altars for Vedic worship using only ropes, stakes, and possibly rods. But what has Vedic altar worship to do with "$a^2 + b^2 = c^2$"?[3]

In his seminal article, "Ritual Origin of Geometry," Seidenberg demonstrates exactly how the Pythagorean theorem was used in creating the falcon-shaped altar used in the Vedic fire ritual, the Agnicayana. The altar was built based upon an aerial measure called a *purusa*! The falcon altar, we are told in the sutra, must be a square with an area of 7.5 square purusas (about 56.25 square feet). A *śulba*, or cord, is used to measure out a purusa (about 7.5 feet) and marked on a section of the cord from an end, and this section is stretched taut between two pegs, one end of the pegged-down cord extending out past a peg, the other end being a meeting point of peg and cord end. Next, the loose cord is stretched back and wrapped around the opposite peg. This peg-to-peg cord stretch is repeated until the desired length is reached. (To achieve the "half purusa," the initial purusa length has been measured by joining both ends of the section and pulling the loop taut by hand and marking the new end with chalk or ink.)

The square is created next—in a manner that we would find odd—by stretching a second cord from the midpoint of the initial 7.5-purusa cord, the end result being a T shape. Then the altar boundary parallel to the initial side is stretched, making an H. The final step is the simple stretching of two boundaries parallel to the central connecting cord. It is not important to trace the subsequent unnecessary (from our practical perspective) steps in creating a square that is 7.5 purusa by 7.5 purusa; we moderns would simply stretch the loose cord, once measured, to make a 7.5-purusa L, and then we'd repeat the process twice more to get a square. Instead, our attention must be focused upon what the Vedic priests did next: They believed that it was necessary to increase the area of the altar by one purusa, without changing the altar's shape!

In this fascinating and illustrative section, we have an important insight that is lost on many: the primal and archetypal rites of ancient humanity in what might be considered a serious contender for the origin of the "perennial tradition" (India). We see that the rites of the gods here encode mathematical forumlae. Specifically in this case, the message is a geometrical formula, and in fact the most famous one. While we are left to speculate on our own as to the divine status of such "gods," what we can divine from this section is the fact that the ritual encodes a mathematical form and functions as a veil for a more axiomatic principle. This seems to suggest a conscious desire to cloak abstract principles from the profane by the priest class, keeping the secrets from the populace through religious fear.

Continuing with this survey of ancient thought, Egyptologist Wim van den Dungen analyzed the Pythagorean and Western conceptions of basic number principles and numerology. Dungen's linked chart also demonstrates the similarity in the various religious traditions through the numerological principles. We see again the theme of hiding numerological doctrines under the divine:

> The first standard is immanent. Using the first ten cardinal numbers of **N**, the set of all natural numbers, the decadic set **N'** {1, 2, 3, 4, 5, 6, 7, 8, 9, 10} is isolated (cf. Pythagorism based on Ancient Egyptian thought and later replicated by the Qabalah). By means of **N'**, all subsequent natural numbers can be derived. Each cardinal number of **N'** is then coupled with a symbol one-to-one. These combinations give form to the famous neo-Platonic formula: *exitus a Deo, reditus in Deum* (outgoing from and return to God). This "numerology" is backed by a process in which the "exit" is an involution (a materialization of spirit) and the "return" an evolution (a spiritualization of matter). Immanence and the realms of process (becoming) prevail.

The second standard is transcendent. Transcendence is approached with negatives (radical *apophatism*). Three kinds emerge: unknowing itself, virtuality (the possible, or {Ø}) and nothingness (the void, or "0"). The first is a nothingness with potential, the second the non-existent (cf. Nature abhors a void). The set of all relevant criteria of measurable differences is given 10 ordinal positions defining 10 dimensions. The logic of Creation (transcendence into immanence and *vice versa*) links with this.[4]

In another influential example, the first-century collection of documents in Koine Greek known as the Corpus Hermeticum relates these numbers to the original Creation act, echoing the same Indian, Hellenic, and Egyptian principles:

I saw in the darkness of the deep, chaotic water without form permeated with a subtle intelligent breath of divine power, Atum's Word fell on fertile waters making them pregnant with all forms. Ordered by the harmony of the Word, the four elements came into being, combining to create the brood of living creatures the fiery element was articulated [ether] as the constellations of the stars, and the gods of the seven heavenly bodies, revolving forever in celestial circles. The Word leapt up from the elements of Nature and reunited with the mind of the Maker, leaving mere matter devoid of intelligence …

In the beginning there is unity. Unity separates into two fundamental forces, which like negative and positive poles of a battery, generate everything. Hermes describes them as Life and Light, which become Mind and Soul. We experience them as thoughts and feelings.[5]

This tradition continued in the Jewish and Christian traditions as van den Dungen expounded, with Kabbalah and gematria. In Kabbalah, the first ten numbers, as in Pythagoreanism, correspond to the divine energies or attributes that shine forth from the One (or God). With this belief, ancient Jewish scholars considered the very letters of the Torah to be divinely inspired, and their particular forms and lexical constructs able to encode secret meanings. Jewish scholar and Kabbalah expert Gershom Scholem defined *gematria* as follows:

> *Gematria* (from Gr. *geometria*), is one of the aggadic hermeneutical rules for interpreting the Torah (in the Baraita of 32 Rules, No. 29). It consists of explaining a word or group of words according to the numerical value of the letters, or of substituting other letters of the alphabet for them in accordance with a set system. Whereas a word is normally employed in this sense of manipulating according to a numerical value, it is sometimes found with the meaning of "calculations" (Avot 3:18) … The use of letters to signify numbers was known to the Babylonians and the Greeks. The first use of gematria occurs in an inscription of Sargon II (727-707 B.C.E.) which states that the king built the wall of Khorsabad 16,283 cubits long to correspond with the numerical value of his name. The use of *gematria* was widespread in the literature of the magi and among interpreters of dreams in the Hellenistic world. [6]

What is relevant to our analysis of Lagarde's comments is that we begin to see that the learned and priest classes would naturally see the pragmatic use of gematria and numerology for conveying messages in a covert fashion. Espionage and statecraft have always gone hand in hand, and the desire of rulers to send encrypted messages is an ancient art. Thus, religious traditions and languages (such as Hebrew and Greek) in which letters also functioned as numbers would naturally serve as a medium for secret communications.

Given that Lagarde's comments involve a peculiar focus on sevens, it might be worthwhile to look not just at the hermeneutical principle of gematria, but at the symbology in scripture of the number seven. Seven serves to convey the idea of completion, finality, and perfection, as the *Oxford Companion to the Bible* relates:

> **Number Symbolism.** In common with most people in the ancient world, the Israelites attached symbolic significance to numbers. So whenever the biblical writers mention a number, it is likely that they had a symbolic meaning in mind; in many cases the numbers must not be taken in their literal sense at all ...
>
> **Seven.** The sum of three plus four, of heaven and of earth, signifies completeness and perfection. There were seven chief heavenly bodies (sun, moon and the five planets known to ancients), seven days of the week, seven archangels. The great festivals lasted seven days, and there were seven weeks between the Passover and the Festival of Weeks (Pentecost). Every seventh year was a Sabbath year, when the land would lie fallow, and Hebrew slaves were allowed to go free; and every fiftieth year was a jubilee, when alienated property had to be returned. The seventh day represented God's completed work (Gen. 2:2-3), and in the Book of Revelation, the seventh seal, trumpet, bowl, etc., represent the completion of God's plan. The seven

spirits of God (Rev. 1-4) represent either the seven archangels, or "all spirits," of the Holy Spirit. Seven churches represent the universal church (Rev. 1:20). It is necessary to forgive, not just seven times, but seventy times seven (Matt. 18:21-22, Gen. 4:24), that is to say, always. [7]

The most famous example of gematria most people are familiar with is the reference in the Apocalypse to 666, the number of the beast. Biblical scholars have long considered it a use of gematria in which John encoded the name of Nero Caesar or another contemporary Roman emperor. Biblical scholar Dr. Kenneth Gentry elucidates of 666:

"This method, called gematria, or geometrical, that is, mathematical, was used by the Jews in exegesis of the Old Testament." The point is clear: cryptograms were common among the ancients, even among Christians. Hence, the gematria in Revelation is not something created *de novo* by John; rather, the idea involved a familiar concept to the ancients. [8]

Another relevant association with 666 is the number squares that can be generated with that give rise to various speculations, but for the purposes of our discussion relate to the topic of magic squares. Biblical scholar E. W. Bullinger gives an example:

Bullinger's number square of "666," which gives 111 in all directions.

The number square is alleged to derive from the geometrical structure of the pattern found on the shell of a tortoise in ancient China (See "The Malekulan Journey of the Dead" by John Layard in Spiritual Disciplines: Papers From the Eranos Yearbooks). Ancient mathematicians associated the number or magic square with various planets and planetary deities and their representative angelic sigils. However, rather than fixating on the religious, it is my thesis that the number square also has a relation to cryptography and the rise of the computer. Since the square gives an ordered regularity, it was reasonable to suppose that a machine might be constructed to calculate and encode. I have written elsewhere of Leibniz's speculations regarding a machine that would mirror the human mind, storing information and mirroring it back. The medieval mythology of the golem also factored into this equation, linking once again gematriaand Kabbalah, where the matrix of external reality itself could be imaged in a 2D virtual realm, which I will touch on later. Before that, consider biblical scholar David Chilton's arrangement of "666" in triangulation in his *The Days of Vengeance*, page 349.[9]

My purpose here is not to speculate as to the identity of an Antichrist, but to look at how the ancient mind viewed numbers and symbols. One can see in these visual pictorials that recall Pythagoreanism the topological principles of mathematical abstraction that would be highly useful for statecraft in constructing ciphers. One of the famous ancient examples of just such a cipher is known as the scytale, used by the Greeks. Singh, in *The Code Book: The Science of Secrecy from Ancient Egypt to Quantum Cryptography*, gives an example of the scytale, a tool used for transposition ciphers, which resembles the tabled structure of a magic square. Given that the Greek alphabet functioned as a number system just as Hebrew did, the jump from magic squares to lettered codes is not a big leap.

It would therefore be natural for ancient people to encode messages in such a fashion.

At this point, it would be requisite to consider more historic examples of cryptography, its origins, and its usages. One of the earliest is found in the writings of Greek historian Herodotus. Herodotus described the Greek danger presented by the invading Persian forces and the need for secret communications to help aid the cause:

> As the danger of discovery was great, there was only one way in which he could contrive to get the message through: this was by scraping the wax off a pair of wooden folding tablets, writing on the wood underneath what Xerxes intended to do, and then covering the message over with wax again. In this way the tablets, being apparently blank, would cause no trouble with the guards along the road. When the message reached its destination, no one was able to guess the secret, until, as I understand, Cleomenes' daughter Gorgo, who was the wife of Leonides, divined and told the others that if they scraped the wax off, they would find something written on the wood underneath. This was done; the message was revealed and read, and afterwards passed on to the other Greeks. [10]

Likewise, in the case of Julius Caesar, we have examples of what would become known as the Caesar Cipher in messages to Cicero. First-century Roman historian Suetonius recounted this transposition process:

> There are also letters of his to Cicero, as well as to his intimates on private affairs, and in the latter, if he had anything confidential to say, he wrote it in

cipher, that is, by so changing the order of the letters
of the alphabet, that not a word could be made out.
If anyone wishes to decipher these, and get at their
meaning, he must substitute the fourth letter of the
alphabet, namely D, for A, and so with the others. [11]

The substitution cipher is the oldest form of encryption, but it
was not immune to being cracked, and this honor fell to the Arabs in
the Middle Ages, who in fact invented the practice of cryptanalysis.
Singh commented:

> This simplicity and strength meant that the
> substitution cipher dominated the art of secret
> writing throughout the first millennium A.D.
> Codemakers had evolved a system for guaranteeing
> secure communication, so there was no need for
> further development—without necessity, there was
> no need for further invention ... The breakthrough
> occurred in the East and required a brilliant
> combination of linguistics, statistics and religious
> devotion.

> Had Arabs been merely familiar with the use
> of monoalphabetic substitution cipher, they
> would not warrant a significant mention in any
> history of cryptography. However, in addition
> to employing ciphers, the Arab scholars were
> also capable of destroying ciphers. They in fact
> invented cryptanalysis, the science of unscrambling
> a message without knowledge of the key. While
> the cryptographer develops new methods of secret
> writing, it is the cryptanalyst who struggles to find
> a weakness in these methods in order to break into
> secret messages. Arabian cryptanalysts succeeded in

finding a method for breaking the monoalphabetic substitution cipher, a cipher that had remained vulnerable for several centuries. [12]

In fact, it was not merely Arabs who were interested in cracking cryptological codes; medieval monastics and members of the Vatican, too, were also skilled in the same arts. Singh explained of the medieval monks who encountered another example of Jewish encoding in the text of Jeremiah:

> Medieval monks were intrigued by the fact that the Old Testament contained deliberate and obvious examples of cryptography. For example, the Old Testament includes pieces of text encrypted with atbash, a traditional form of Hebrew substitution cipher. Atbash involves taking each letter, noting the number of places it is from the beginning of the alphabet, and replacing it with a letter that is an equal number of places from the end of the alphabet. In English this would mean that a, at the beginning of the alphabet, is replaced by Z, at the end of the alphabet, b is replaced by Y, and so on. The term atbash itself hints at the substitution it describes, because it consists of the first letter of the Hebrew alphabet, aleph, followed by the last letter taw, and then there is the second letter, beth, followed by the second to last letter shin. An example of atbash appears in Jeremiah 25: 26 and 51: 41, where "Babel" is replaced by the word "Sheshach"; the first letter of Babel is beth, the second letter of the Hebrew alphabet, and this is replaced by shin, the second-to-last letter; the second letter of Babel is also beth, and so it too is replaced by shin; and the last letter of Babel is lamed, the twelfth letter of the

Hebrew alphabet, and this is replaced by kaph, the twelfth-to-last letter. [13]

Renaissance Europe was awash in intrigues and subterfuges that often called for the use of encryption. It is at this point we should shift back to the esoteric and consider fifteenth/sixteenth-century German polymath Cornelius Agrippa, considered the father of Western hermeticism. Agrippa was accused of being a conjurer, but he was also learned in the arts I have described here. The Renaissance brought classical learning back into fashion, and as a result, the desire to crack hidden codes by means of linguistics and numerology and gematria became, once again, *en vogue*. Agrippa provided an excellent example of the associations and connections of numerology, theology, alchemy, and techne. Agrippa wrote:

> God himself though he be only one in Essence, yet hath diverse names, which expound not his diverse Essences or Deities, but certain properties flowing from him, by which names he doth pour down, as it were by certain Conduits on us and all his creatures many benefits and diverse gifts; ten of these Names we have above described, which also *Hierom* reckoneth up to *Marcella*. *Dionysius* reckoneth up forty five names of God and Christ. The *Mecubales* of the Hebrews from a certain text of Exodus, derive seventy-two names, both of the Angels and of God, which they call the name of seventy two letters, and *Schemhamphores*, that is, the expository; but others proceeding further, out of all places of the Scripture do infer so many names of God as the number of those names is: but what they signifie is altogether unknown to us: From these therefore, besides those which we have reckoned up before, is the name of the Divine Essence, *Eheia*

äéàà, which *Plato*translates wn, from hence they call God TO ON, others O UNthat is the being. *Hu* àåä is another name revealed to *Esay*, signifying the Abysse of the Godhead, which the Greeks translate TAUTON, the Latins, himself the same ...

Which the Ancient Doctors of the Hebrews have especially observed, who were wont to do many wonderful things by words; the *Pythagorians* [Pythagoreans] also have shewed, how to cure very wonderfully the diseases both of body and mind, with certain words; we read also, that *Orpheus,* being one of the Argonauts diverted a most fierce storm by certain words; in like manner that *Apollonius,* by certain words whispered, raised up a dead maide at *Rome*; and *Philostratus* reporteth that some did by certain words call up *Achilles* Ghost; and *Pausanias* relates, that in *Lydia* in the Cities of *Hiero-Cesarea* and *Hypepis,* were two temples consecrated to the Goddess whom they called *Persica,* in both of which when divine service was ended, a certain Magitian [magician], after he had laid dry wood upon the Altar, and in his native language had sang 'Hymnes, and pronounced certain barbarous words, out of a book which he held in his hand, presently the dry wood, no fire being put to it, was seen to be kindled, and burn most clearly. Also *Serenus Samonicus* delivereth amongst the precepts of Physick, that if this name *Abracadabra* be written, as is here expressed, *viz.* diminishing letter after letter backward, from the last to the first, it will cure the Hemitritean Fever or any other, if the sheet of paper or parchment be hanged about the neck,

and the disease will by little and little decline and
pass away.

a b r a c a d a b r a

a b r a c a d a b r

a b r a c a d a b

a b r a c a d a

a b r a c a d

a b r a c a

a b r a c

a b r a

a b r

a b

a^{14}

The pyramidal structure of *abracadabra* is reminiscent of the
triangulation of 666 or the *tetraktys* (a triangular figure consisting
of ten points in four rows). The tetraktys is not merely an encoded
hermetic message; it is also a geometric form. As an undergrad, I read
a large portion of volume 1 of nineteenth-century researcher into
secret societies Charles Heckethorn's *The Secret Societies of All Ages*.
One aspect that came to the fore was the pigpen cipher. Not only
is this an ancient method of secret communication, but the nine-
squared box can also enclose all the letters of the English alphabet
as well as the first nine numerals (which make up all numbers). It

is easy to see how the magic square, the emergence of linguistics, number forms, the pigpen cipher, and various esoteric ideas all intertwine. Yet aside from the religious and esoteric views, there is also the ever-present use of these ideas by the state for secret communications.

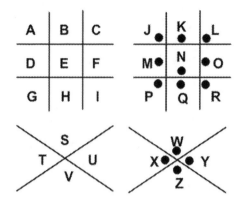

The classic pigpen cipher. When the "X" is laid over the #, the entire English alphabet and the first nine numerals are present.

Fast forward now to Renaissance England and think of Dr. John Dee, the first 007 as well as court astrologer for Queen Elizabeth I. Dee was involved in many intrigues, one of which was cryptology. However, as National Security Agency (NSA) scholar Leslie Rutledge explains, not a very good one. In fact, despite the many legends of Dee as a conjurer talking to the dead with his crystal ball, the evidence seems to weigh in on Dee as a con man, calling to mind Agrippa. Regardless, Dee is another example of the intersect of the esoteric and cryptography. Rutledge wrote in his essay "John Dee: Consultant to Queen Elizabeth":

> Mathematics lifts the heart above the heavens by invisible lines, and by its immortal beams melteth the reflection of light incomprehensible, and so procureth joy and perfection unspeakable.
> -Dr. John Dee citing Plato

The book was notorious, I just now pointed out. Trithemius, the Abbot of Spaheim, began to write it in the year 1500, and he sent a partial copy of it to a clerical friend in another religious establishment. But unknown to Trithemius, his friend had died. His friend's abbot opened the correspondence, and he was appalled. "Secret writings," he read, "will reveal secrets not found by ordinary means." And there was more. In order to send a secret message, you make an image of a planetary angel, speak the message over it at a moment determined by complicated astrological calculations, wrap the image up with an image of the addressee, and bury the images. This network of planetary angels could always be used for messages—and even for thought transference.

Cryptography, even of this heavenly sort, was not just a means of disguising messages; it was the medium through which intelligence from the spirit world might be transmitted. The secrets of the universe—the philosopher's stone. "The elixir of life-might be received in a heavenly cipher, like the obscure oracles of Delphi." The abbot denounced Trithemius as a conjuror, trafficking with spirits, and he lost his clearance. Although he stopped all work on the *Steganographia*, the manuscript of it appears to have circulated as an underground classic for nearly a century until Dee copied it in 1563. It was finally published in Frankfurt, near the end of Dee's life, in 1606.

It was, you see, the supernatural context of the *Steganography* which attracted attention. Heads of state—or adventurers of all sorts could be persuaded that secrets of the future, hidden in the stars, and the marvelous formulae for prolonging life and for converting base metals into gold were knowable—and might be revealed by the supernal powers in cipher. It is hard perhaps to realize, but rational and wholly illusory notions like this could and did exist in the 16ᵗʰ Century scientific mind. Even Copernicus did not disbelieve in astrology. There were two gates to the other world. There was a gate of horn, through which came the rational finding which would lead to our times, and an extraordinary perception of the nature of man and his world. But there was also a gate of ivory, through which dreams and illusions came.[15]

According to Rutledge, Dee was not successful at this magical, astrological means of cryptography. However, the essay does relate the story of Dee mentioning the ability to project images through screens, which I have noted elsewhere appears to relate to the seminal idea of the computer, and it is to Leibniz that we once again return. Leibniz's idea of a *characteristica universalis* was instrumental in the development of calculation machines arising from the project of a universal logic for all phenomena. Nikolay Milkov, fellow at The Center for Philosophy of Science in Pittsburgh explained:

The first variant of Leibniz's project for a new language was set out in a letter from Marin Mersenne to Descartes. In fact, Mersenne's idea was that of pasigraphy, a general language that helps one to understand all languages. In his reply to Mersenne of 11 November 1629, Descartes found this project rather interesting; however, he suggested a much wider variant of it: a project for ideography that mirrors human thoughts. This ideography would be connected with a mathesis universalis that could conceive of anything thinkable as a calculation. — The greatest advantage of such a language would be the assistance it would give to men's judgment, representing matters so clearly that it would be almost impossible to go wrong. [16]

Amazingly, Leibniz wrote of a possible "imagined" machine:

It must be confessed, moreover, that perception and that which depends on it, are inexplicable by mechanical causes, which is by figures and motions. And, supposing that there were a machine so constructed as to think, feel and have perception, we could conceive of as enlarged and yet preserving the same proportions, so that we might enter into it as into a mill. And this granted, we should only find on visiting it, pieces which push one against another, but never anything by which to explain a perception. This must be sought for, therefore, in the simple substance and not in the composite or in the machine. Furthermore, nothing but this (namely perception and their changes) can be found in the simple substance. It is also in this alone that all the internal activities of simple substances can consist. The name of *entelechies* might be given to all simple substances or created monads, for they have within themselves a certain perfection; there is a certain sufficiency which makes them sources of internal activities, and so to speak, incorporeal automata. [17]

In Leibniz, the father of calculus, the convergence of symbology and earlier cryptographic and esoteric ideas combine to produce a further exposition and advance on the idea of creating a logic machine that functioned like a mind. While my intention here is not to delve into the history of the computer, it is worth considering that the history of cryptography and cryptanalysis is directly connected to the emergence of the idea of the computer. Only in a world in which mathematical principles are "mirrored" from the realm of forms to our external world could such a machine function. If you are reading this digitally, you are in fact using the very thing described—a machine that transmits encrypted information from one person to another.

British physicist Paul Davies related an interesting story about the advancement of computers by Los Alamos Laboratory scientists that also recalls Leibniz's walk-in computer based on the same principle of universal logic and a *characteristica universalis*. This time, however, the purpose is to mimic life. Davies explained:

> The fact that universal computers can simulate each other has some important implications. On the practical level it means that, properly programmed and with enough memory space bolted on, a modest IBM PC can perfectly imitate, say, a powerful Cray computer as far as output (not speed) is concerned. In fact, a universal computer need be nowhere as sophisticated as an IBM PC. It might consist of nothing more than a checkerboard and a supply of checkers! Such a system was first studied by the mathematicians Stanislaw Ulam and John von Neumann in the 1950s as an example of what is called "game theory." Ulam and von Neumann were working at the Los Alamos National Laboratory, where the Manhattan atomic bomb project was conducted … He [von Neumann] was fascinated

to know whether a machine could in principle be built that is capable of reproducing itself, and if so, what its structure might be. If such a von Neumann machine is possible, then we would be able to understand the principles that enable biological organisms to reproduce themselves. The basis of von Neumann's analysis was the construction of a "universal constructor" analogous to a "universal computer." This would be a machine programmed to produce anything, much as a Turing machine can be programmed to execute any computable mathematical operation.[18]

In Leibniz, the principle of gnomonicity is applied to the monads, and with computers, supercomputers, and personal computers, the same gnomonic principle applies. This is reminiscent of Chilton's triangulation of 666 in which removing one layer leaves a smaller, yet same, shape. The point here is that the gnomonic principle is based on the mirroring principle—that what is true in thought, logic, and nature is also true from the macro scale to the micro scale. It is in this way that the secrets of nature encode the rites of the gods. What we see at the subatomic level mirrors what we see in galaxies and the solar system. The book of Wisdom 11:20 states, "But you have disposed all things by measure and number and weight." However, that scientists will create a "sentient" computer is impossible, given the objective truth of Gödel's theorems and the impossibility of accounting for all infinite potentialities. AI scientist and semiotician Douglas Hofstadter commented:

> Clearly there is much more going on in typefaces than meets the eye–literally. The shape of letterform is a surface manifestation of deep mental abstractions. It is determined by conceptual considerations and balances that no finite set of merely geometric knobs

could capture. Underneath or behind each instance of "A" there lurks a concept, a Platonic entity, a spirit, This Platonic entity is not an elegant shape such as the Univers A, not a template with a finite number of knobs, not a topological or grouping-theoretical invariant in some mathematical heaven, but a mental abstraction—a different sort of beast. Each instance of the "A" spirit reveals something new about the spirit without ever exhausting it. The mathematization of such a spirit would be a machine with a specific set of knobs on it, defining all its "loci of variability" for once and for all. I have tried to show that to expect this is simply not reasonable.[19]

In other words, there is clearly something beyond the letter on paper, the letter spoken, and the letter in the mind. Something invariant and not bound by time must link all these particular instantiations, and thus by the wayside falls reductionist materialism (though they are almost incapable of grasping this). The danger is not from sentient supercomputers as presented in some ridiculous Hollywood blockbuster, but from the actual supercomputer spy grid that was erected under the auspices of the Cold War. In his 1982 book on the National Security Agency (NSA), James Bamford mentioned a curiously titled cryptographic program:

> The timing could not have been better for IBM, which submitted for consideration its Lucifer cipher. Labeled by David Kahn "the tiniest known 'cipher machine' ever produced," Lucifer actually consisted of a thumbnail-sized silicon "chip" containing an extremely complex integrated circuit. The "key" to the cipher was a long string of bits—0s and 1s— the combination of which would vary from user

to user ... From the very beginning, the NSA had taken an enormous interest in Project Lucifer. [20]

First, remove the chip in your all-seeing eye.

Along the same lines, mathematician Calvin Clawson expanded on this program in his 1996 book, *Mathematical Mysteries: The Beauty and Magic of Numbers*, which shows the level of advanced surveillance that existed in the 1990s! Clawson wrote:

> The German version of this [cipher] machine was called the Enigma, on of which was obtained by the British. The Enigma, in conjunction with cryptanalysis techniques allowed the British to decipher many German messages, which significantly altered World War II's outcome ... Companies and governments worldwide are not adopting the public-key cipher system. RSA Data Security, Inc. has grown to be the leading cryptographic marketing company in the nation ...

> With the phenomenal growth in the use of public-key encryption methods, such as the RSA system, we might be led to believe that public key codes will soon become the national, or even world standard. However, the U.S. Government has been fighting to avoid such a situation. The National Security Agency of the U.S. Government is responsible for breaking the codes of foreign governments- they are our secret spy agency. But the NSA knows it cannot break the public key-codes ... No wonder the NSA is upset about the RSA success story.

> The government has not been idle, and is now working on a competing system to public-key

encryption. In 1987, Congress authorized NIST to develop an acceptable encryption system that would satisfy the needs of user privacy, yet allow law enforcement agencies and the NSA to decipher transmitted messages. This effort became the Capstone Project. Under Capstone, a computer chip, called a Clipper Chip, would be manufactured and installed in computers that interface with the U.S. Government.[21]

Lucifer and Capstone: names undoubtedly imbued with esoteric significance. Even in my semi demythologizing project in this book, I am unable to avoid esoteric notions as we move into the 20th century. It seems that cryptography, which developed from ancient message writing and gematria and eventually produced the Enigma machine of World War II and the computer itself, is still deeply related to occult ideas. Does that mean we can decode Lagarde's cipher? We may not have all the keys for her message, but what we do have is a grounding in the understanding that Lagarde is primarily using her message as a message of statecraft as old as the art of language itself. Whether one regards the "magic" as real or not, one thing we can be certain of is statecraft and cryptography.

What of gods then? Must we conclude that it is all statecraft and sciencia and techne, people in search of secret ways of communicating and being, apart from anything religious? No, not at all. People are more religious than ever, only their gods have changed. Instead, just as we plumb the depths of nature and science, like Hofstadter's comments on the Platonic nature of signs and symbols, we find that each new revelation conceals as much as it reveals. We are not left with a dry, barren Enlightenment rationalism; neither are we returning to an ancient superstition. We are involved in the ever-progressing revelation of reality that spirals for all eternity, as St. Gregory of Nyssa wrote, up eternally into the divine. It's not dialectics; it's a principle of unification and synthesis and not in a

Hegelian sense. (Hegel's view was based on dialectical tension.) This eternal learning constantly removes superstition as it simultaneously invites us deeper into theological mystery. It is the acceptance of paradox, which is very different from a contradiction in philosophy that is the appropriate (and Eastern) attitude.

Notes:

1 ?
2 Simon Singh, *The Code Book: The Science of Secrecy from Ancient Egypt to Quantum Cryptography* (), 12.
3 James Kelley. "Prajapati Purusa and Vedic Altar Construction"
4 Eric van den Dungen, "Tabularm Esotericum"
5 Timothy Freke and Peter Gandy, *The Hermetica* (),13–14, 35.
6 Gershom Scholem, *Kabbalah* (), 337.
7 (*Oxford Guide to the Bible*, 562–3)
8 (*Before Jerusalem Fell: Dating of the Book of Revelation*, pg. 196)
9 on page 286 of his *Number in Scripture*:
10 (*The Histories*, Bk. V)
11 (Suetonius, *The Lives of the Caesars*, "Caesar," No. 56)
12 (Ibid., 15) (but it's not Ibid.)
13 (Singh, *The Code Book*, pg. 26)
14 Cornelius Agrippa, *Three Books of Occult Philosophy*, Bk. III, XI
15 ?
16 (Nikolay Milkov, "Leibniz Project for a *Characteristica Universalis* in Relation to the Early Analytical Philosophy," pg. 2)
17 (pg. 536)
18 Paul Davies, *The Mind of God: The Scientific Basis for a Rational World* (), 111–2.
19 Douglas Hofstadter, *Metamagical Themas: Questing for the Essence of Mind and Pattern* (), 279.
20 James Bamford, *Puzzle Palace* (), 435.
21 Clawson, *Mathematical Mysteries* (),186, 199–200)

CHAPTER 14

Hume and Kant: Synthetic A Priori

The famed eighteenth-century skeptic-empiricist, David Hume concluded his *An Inquiry Concerning Human Understanding* by declaring:

> When we run over libraries, persuaded of these
> [his] principles, what havoc must we make? If
> we take in our hand any volume; of divinity or
> school metaphysics, for instance; let us ask; does it
> contain any abstract reasoning concerning quantity
> or number? No. Does it contain any experimental
> reasoning concerning matter of fact and existence?
> No. Commit it then to the flames: for it can contain
> nothing but sophistry and illusion.[1]

The arguments from Hume's *Inquiry* admittedly forced Immanuel Kant to awaken from his "dogmatic slumbers" of uncritical metaphysical assumptions.[2]

My purpose here is to examine the reasons for these bold statements and to consider the chief epistemological and metaphysical point of contention between both philosophers. Hume's project was one of critical analysis. His goal was to question the assumptions philosophers had hitherto used to construct elaborate metaphysical systems. His principal example of criticism, possibly the most foundational assumption of speculative theorists in his day, was the concept of causality. Causality had been taken as a foundational axiom of reality: from Aristotle to the Schoolmen to Leibniz, causality was assumed to be a self-evident, universal, necessary law of reality. Hume posited, however, that causality is not grounded in any rational, a priori argumentation; rather, it is entirely unfounded. He wrote, in a word, then, that every effect is a distinct event from its cause. It could not, therefore, be discovered in the cause, and the first invention or conception of it, a priori, must be entirely arbitrary. And even after it is suggested, the conjunction of it with the cause must appear entirely arbitrary since there are always many other effects, which, to reason, must seem fully as consistent and natural. In vain, therefore, should we pretend to determine any single event, or infer any cause or effect, without the assistance of observation and experience.[3]

There is no basis in experience for one event following necessarily upon another, Hume argued, and thus causality cannot be rationally justified. In other words, no contradiction is involved in denying the supposed necessity of causality; but a statement's denial is what proves it to be necessary if the denial results in a manifest contradiction. Thus, because there is no contradiction involved in denying the supposed necessity of causality, its denial does not amount to a contradiction. If no contradiction is involved in denying the necessity of causality, then causality is not a priori.

If causality is not a priori, Hume thought, our belief in the necessary connection between two events must be a posteriori, and therefore a product not of rational justification, but of psychological custom or habit. As Runes's *Dictionary of Philosophy* notes,

> As knowledge [for Hume] consists in relations of ideas in virtue of resemblance, and as the only relation which involves the connection of different existences and the inference of one existence from

another is that of cause and effect, and as there
is no resemblance necessary between cause and
effect, causal inference is in no case experientially
or formally certifiable ... the necessity of causal
connection must be explained psychologically.[4]

Hume can then declare "that the sun will not rise tomorrow is no
less intelligible a proposition, and implies no more contradiction than
the affirmation, that it will rise."[5] Causality and similar believed-
to-be a priori maxims had been the very foundation upon which
previous metaphysics and foundationalist epistemology had relied:
without a priori judgments of experience, metaphysics as a science
would appear impossible. It is this apparently irresolvable dilemma
that drove Hume to declare that the volumes of the speculators
and schoolmen are only worthy of flames. Metaphysics, for Hume,
was an impossibility, which landed him in full skepticism. Further,
Hume's removal of the previously assumed inductive and causal
principles seemed to destroy the rational justification for doing
natural science: it was here that Kant picked up the issue, seeking
to save science.

Immanuel Kant, as I have mentioned, was awakened by Hume's
critique somewhat late in life and began a project he would title a
"Copernican revolution" in philosophy. Kant sought to solve the
problem of metaphysics by constructing his system of critical or
transcendental idealism by which the pitfalls of skepticism could
be avoided. He restated Hume's question in a more formal fashion
by asking how synthetic a priori judgments could be possible; that
is, how are a priori statements that contain expansive information
about experience not contained in the subject itself justifiably held to
be universal and necessary? Following Hume's devastating critique,
Kant admitted they appeared to be impossible: it was here that Kant
proposed a brilliant solution to Hume's question.

Rather than considering causality as an organizing principle
of nature, something metaphysical, causality is a universally and

necessarily existing category imposed by the mind upon reality. As such, it is a precondition for the intelligibility of experience. Synthetic a priori judgments are shown to be rationally justified by the fact that they are preconditions for intelligibility. Kant wrote:

> This is, therefore, the result of all our foregoing inquiries: "All synthetic principles a prior are nothing more than principles of possible experience" and can never be referred to things in themselves, but only to appearances as objects of experience. And hence pure mathematics as well as pure natural science can never be referred to anything more than mere appearances, and can only represent either than which makes experience in general possible, or else that which, as it is derived from these principles must always be capable of being represented in some possible experience.[6]

In other words, certain mental categories must characterize objects of experience for the entirety of our experience to be coherent. These a priori intuitions, such as space and time, for example, are presupposed in any knowledge or act and are demonstrated by being principles of all possible experience. To deny the pure intuitions of space, time, and/or causality would be to make experience unintelligible.

In this way, then, Kant believed he had found a method for the natural sciences, which used metaphysical assumptions, to be saved from Hume's devastating critique. Where Hume had offered only a negative criticism without any attempt at solving the issue, Kant posited a solution. The question that remains is whether Kant's answer was entirely sufficient: while providing undoubtedly brilliant insights, does his construction ultimately provide a salvation for science, or is it merely psychologized?

Yale religion professor Louis Dupre made an excellent point on the difficult intellectual position post-Enlightenment humanity is left in:

> This removal of transcendence fundamentally affected the conveyance of meaning. Whereas previously meaning had been established in the very act of Creation by a wise God, it now fell upon the human mind to interpret a cosmos, the structure of which had ceased to be given as intelligible. Instead of being an integral part of the cosmos, the person became its source of meaning. Mental life separated from cosmic being: as meaning-giving "subject," the mind became the spiritual substratum of all reality. Only what it objectively constituted would count as real. Thus reality split into two separate spheres: that of the mind, which contained all intellectual determinations, and that of all other beings, which received them.[7]

Although this would seem to be a commentary only on the state of humanity post-Enlightenment, I believe there is also a powerful argument implicit therein that hints at the solution to the chief epistemological problem of Hume and Kant.

Numerous problems arise when an individual's mind is made the final reference point of predication. In other words, individuals are cut off from the totality of reality, including what they refer to as transcendence, meaning predication cannot be coherent. If existence precedes essence, to use the existential dictum, meaning loses all meaning outside the individual subject. Kant believed that he could speak meaningfully about appearances but not about the in-itself, the noumenal realm. I am in full agreement, then, with Hegel on this point of critique; the epistemological turn in Enlightenment philosophers ends up only giving a semblance of knowledge.

Kant assumed, first of all, that all other minds naturally work in the way his prolegomena and *Critique of Pure Reason* explained. I realize that Kant gave what he conceived to be necessary categories for the possibility of experience. At first glance, this seems beyond critique. My insight, however, is that Kant seems to have overstepped the bounds of the phenomenal/noumenal distinction at this very point. His position presupposed that all minds work according to the structure proposed by his system: nature simply constitutes the mind to so operate.

However, do we not have here a synthetic a priori statement that cannot be justified? For, to say that all minds work in this fashion is to make an a priori statement that expands upon the idea of minds and their actions. Had Kant not boldly stepped over into the noumenal realm when he spoke of "minds," assuming other minds to work in this same fashion? Remember that Kant conceived of his pure intuitions and categories as necessary. My point is therefore proven by the fact that another's mind can never be given to Kant in his experience of appearances. But, according to Kant, the realm of absolute certainty is the realm of appearances (the phenomenal).

Another way to take this criticism is the path that Hegel took. I said previously that to cut the individual off from the totality of existence is to eliminate meaning. Such is precisely the criticism that Hegel gave of a Kantian-type approach. How can we make sense of a statement of fact if we cannot attain to the in-itself? How can conceptual meaning be correctly attributed to and predicated of an object of experience without relating it to the universal concept? But when we are dealing in universal concepts, we are stepping outside the realm of appearances only. Language itself seems to presuppose universals, as does mathematics. Hegel was absolutely correct that we must return to metaphysics and the in-itself if we are to make sense of our experience. In fact, the Kantian enterprise even presupposes this point when it attempts to speak about the noumenal at all. Even a purely negative statement such as "the noumenal cannot be known" is still a universal-truth statement about the noumenal. It at least assumes the noumenal exists.

I do not follow Hegel into a pantheistic, dialectical monism, however. I agree that we need the absolute mind to stand behind, if you will, the objects of experience, giving them underlying meaning. For experience to be meaningful, it must have essence precede existence, or else our experience loses itself in an endless sea of unconnected, meaningless events. The human self cannot be the unifying principle since the self cannot attain to the omniscience necessary to say anything meaningful about a thing (to the universal, that is). It seems to me, then, that philosophy has come full circle from the ancients and scholastics. Hegel realized this, but I do not think his answer is coherent. The solution is likely to be found in a return to the approach of St. Anselm's project of attempting to find a necessary proof for God.[8] I do not say this merely because of personal preferences for religious philosophy; rather, I say it because I think this move of Hegel to seek to return to metaphysics and his insight into the need to relate the particular to the whole to say anything meaningful about an object is the right approach.

It is here that I see something unique in the traditional conception of a revelation-based epistemology that hints at answering the dilemma that even Hegel leaves us with. In God there is an ultimate unity and an ultimate plurality, but rather than an impersonal thought of Aristotle or Hegel, the omniscient absolute is also personal. I believe this is key because it seems that meaning presupposes personality, as opposed to impersonal, brute factuality that somehow gives rise to "meaning," and I suspect this relates to the idea of the logos.

The problems presented by Hume and Kant (and Hegel) point us to the following needs: It seems we assume many philosophical issues relating to linguistics and meaning in order to predicate anything at all, and this prior meaning seems to need to emanate from beyond ourselves. We need to relate it beyond ourselves because the finite needs to relate the concept to the infinite to make its predication "stick" to the object, if you will.

We seem to need this ultimate universal to contain the universals in a personal, mental way and not merely as an impersonal force. We also need to return to analogy in speaking of this absolute in order to be able to know about this absolute. Indeed, when I say *absolute* in the realm of linguistic and interpersonal discourse, as you read this book, it seems to assume a kind of analogical mode whereby you seem to understand what I mean by *absolute*, and yet you and I are both finite.[9] In doing this, however, we would be reversing the project of the nominalists and reintroducing, at least to some degree, the chain-of-being model, which is bound up with the notion of predicating things of God on the basis of a *via negativa* analogy. We must return to the external transcendent, but the transcendent must be accessible to the finite mind.

Notes:

1   David Hume, *An Inquiry Concerning Human Understanding*
2   ?
3   ?
4   Runes' *Dictionary of Philosophy*
5   Hume
6   ?
7   Louis Dupre
8   ?
9   ?

CHAPTER 15

Horkheimer, Adorno, and the Frankfurt School

Max Horkheimer and Theodore W. Adorno, key figures of the Frankfurt School of Marxist Critical Theory, founded in 1918 in the Wiemar Republic, wrote in their landmark work, "Dialectic of Enlightenment," that "myth is already enlightenment, and enlightenment reverts to mythology."[1] By this, the authors meant that the historical progression of the Enlightenment tradition has actually subverted its original intentions of, as Francis Bacon wrote, making humanity the sovereign of nature, and has actually produced the opposite: barbarity and domination of the social nature in fascism and Stalinism.[2] In response to this, later Frankfurt School writer, Jurgen Habermas, responded to Horkheimer and Adorno with an interesting counter-critique. The purpose of this paper will be to examine Horkheimer and Adorno's criticism of Enlightenment and Habermas' response.

The project that Horkeimer and Adorno engaged in is correctly titled an "immanent critique" and called by Habermas "ideology critique." This type of critique arises out of the work of Kant and Hegel. In this approach, a system or ideology is investigated internally to see whether its presuppositions are consistent with one another. If they are not, then the system is considered self-refuting. Thus,

Jay Dyer

Horkheimer and Adorno made the case that the Enlightenment tradition fails the test, and the inheritors of the Enlightenment tradition, namely the Vienna Circle positivists and nominalists, are involved in promulgating a self-destructive, self-refuting ideology.[3]

Horkheimer and Adorno set forth their case in the essay "The Concept of Enlightenment." They held that Enlightenment thinking had displayed several major motifs: demythologizing the natural world through knowledge and control, and dominating that demythologized nature through autonomous, instrumental reason. These motifs are interconnected, and actually interact and affect one another in a dialectical fashion.

First, they argue that the Enlightenment tradition has, from humankind's beginning, been bound up with myth. A study of the social evolution of ancient societies demonstrates, according to Horkheimer and Adorno, that myth actually arises as a response to mystery and the domination of humankind by the natural world. Thus, we can see that, in the earliest known human societies, the mythological scheme actually produces a kind of classification, a seeking for origins, and reductionism, though not self-consciously. In other words, just like Enlightenment, "myth seeks to explain."[4] Enlightenment, however, since Bacon, Kant, Hume, and even the positivists, has failed to recognize this dialectical relationship. Instead, for the Enlightenment, anything that cannot be resolved into numbers, and ultimately into one, is illusion; modern positivism consigns it to poetry. Unity remains the watchword from Parmenides to Russell. All gods and qualities must be destroyed.[5]

Second, just as Enlightenment is occupied with the fetish of mathematical quantification of all reality, the ancient world displayed the same type of attempt at domination of nature by magic. Though there are obvious differences between the two, magic sought at least to control and manipulate the natural world: "Magic, like science, is concerned with ends, but it pursues them through mimesis ..."[6] In fact, the solar, patriarchal myth was a type of enlightenment seen in its historical context.[7] Enlightenment's attempt at classifying all

190

events as cause-and-effect relations, which has developed into a sort of hard, materialistic determinism, also had its forerunner in mythological traditions. It was precisely the concept of fate that attempted to classify events as causal and somehow rational.

What is evident in these examples is people's attempt to become liberated from the perceived conflict between themselves and the natural world; they are alienated from nature. In response, they seek reconciliation through domination of nature. Domination, however, does not just occur in the realm of nature. It also occurs in the social realm. What develops out of this attempt to control nature, socially speaking, is patriarchy and hierarchy. The chiefs and heads will protect the tribe from outside forces contingent upon submission to the headship of the hierarchy.

Third, there is also domination in terms of the inner desires and urges of the individual. People must repress their instincts and natural drives if they are to survive. Horkheimer and Adorno used Homer's character Odysseus as the preeminent example of the emergence of the archetypal enlightened man who must battle nature, suppress his desires, and return home to his position of patriarchal ruler.[8]

What has happened, then, in the modern, enlightened, monopolistic capitalist world, according to Horkheimer and Adorno, is that rationality is meaningless as an objective reality: the positivists have destroyed their own worldview through eliminating meaning itself. Monopolistic structures have emerged that attempt to move all things toward a generic standardization and unification in which thought itself is seen as a mere technological tool that in relation to the whole, is irrational and serves only to appear rational in reifying the dominating structure (purposive rationality). Self-preservation is all that is salvaged from the old order; the system exists only to perpetuate itself. What has resulted in Horkheimer and Adorno's analysis is a kind of Neitzschian power struggle. Thus, Enlightenment dissolves the power it was supposed to give and has turned "into an outright deception of the masses."[9]

Their successor in the Frankfurt School, Jurgen Habermas, did not share their negative appraisal of the Enlightenment tradition. From the outset of his essay-lecture, "The Entwinement of Myth and Enlightenment: Horkheimer and Adorno," Habermas set the stage for the type of critical response he would offer:

> On their [Horkheimer and Adorno] analysis, it is no longer possible to place hope in the liberating force of enlightenment. Inspired by Benjamin's ironic hope of the hopeless, they still do not want to relinquish the now paradoxical labor of conceptualization. [10]

In other words, Habermas would be giving an ideology critique of critical theory itself. Habermas proceeded by first restating the central theses of Horkheimer and Adorno, summarizing the major arguments in *The Dialectic of Enlightenment*: the attempt at disenchanting the natural world and the collapse of metaphysics and normative standards, the rise of purely instrumental reason and the result—the reign of scientism. [11]

As I have mentioned, Habermas disagreed with Horkheimer and Adorno: he thought they had gone too far and had themselves fallen prey to critique, but before going into this, he laid out some preliminary disagreements. Habermas thought *The Dialectic of Enlightenment* failed "to do justice to the rational content of cultural modernity that was captured in bourgeoise ideals (and also instrumentalized along with them)." [12] Habermas meant here the progress achieved by capitalism and self-reflective modern science, universalistic foundations of law and morality, and constitutional and democratic governments, along with avant-garde art. [13] Thus, Habermas described Horkheimer and Adorno's work using the words *incomplete, one-sided,* and *oversimplified.* [14]

The pith of Habermas's response lies in his brilliant turning of critical theory on its own head. Habermas explained that critical theory had as its goal the enlightenment of Enlightenment about itself.[15] Therefore, according to Habermas, "ideology critique fails to have anything in reserve to which it might appeal."[16] It is this fact that has rendered *The Dialectic of Enlightenment* the description "black." Habermas wrote:

> Horkheimer and Adorno regard the foundations of ideology critique as shattered—and they would still like to hold on to the basic figure of the enlightenment. So what enlightenment has perpetuated on myth, they apply to the process of enlightenment as a whole. Inasmuch as it turns against reason as the foundation of its own validity, critique becomes total. How is the totalization and independence of critique to be understood?[17]

When critique becomes total, it must include itself, since critique is a product of enlightenment, since it's a dialectic relationship. When critique becomes total, "reason itself becomes suspected of the baneful confusion of power and validity claims, but still with the intent of enlightening."[18]

Habermas also thought that Horkheimer and Adorno had not just borrowed the methodology of critique from Neitzsche. Habermas thought they had sold enlightened modernity short, since they have followed Neitzsche only in perceiving everywhere a "binding of reason and domination, of power and validity."[19] Habermas outlined several point-for-point similarities with Neitzsche, principally in seeing art, the informed aesthetic judgment, as the sole organ of knowledge and hope of meaning.[20] Habermas proceeded to give Neitzsche the same critical approach he had given Horkheimer and Adorno:

> However, if thinking can no longer operate in the element of truth, or validity claims in general, contradiction and criticism lose their meaning. *To*

contradict, to negate, now has only the sense of *"wanting to be different."* Neitzsche cannot really be satisfied with this in his critique of culture. The latter is not supposed to be merely a form of agitation, but *to demonstrate* why it is false or incorrect or bad to recognize the sovereignty of the ideals of science and universalistic morality, which are inimical to life. But once all predicates concerning validity are devaluated, once it is power and not validity claims that are expressed in value appraisals—by what criterion shall critique still be able to discriminate between a power that *deserves* to be esteemed and one that *deserves* to be devaluated?[21]

Thus, Neitzsche himself, whom Horkheimer and Adorno relied heavily upon in *The Dialectic of Enlightenment*, was prey also to self-refutation by critical theory.

In response to this, Habermas thought Horkheimer and Adorno became "purists" in seeking for Enlightenment ideals in too Platonic a fashion. He wrote:

But they know, or they can know, that this idealization is only necessary because convictions are formed and confirmed in a medium that is not "pure" and not removed from the world of appearances in the style of Platonic Ideas. Only a discourse that admits this might break the spell of mythic thinking without incurring the loss of the light radiating from the semantic potentials also preserved in myth.[22]

In other words, understanding the dialectical method, Horkheimer and Adorno should not have expected such immediate results, perhaps. They should have known that historical materialism and discourse must admit imperfection; the only way to overcome this is universal pragmatics.

In conclusion, while it must be admitted that Max Horkheimer and Theodor W. Adorno have given a brilliant and insightful criticism of Enlightenment thinking and its modern products of positivism and scientism, Habermas's response must also be taken into account; it, in an equally brilliant fashion, points out the critical flaw immanent in critical theory. In the final assessment, it seems that Habermas showed the inconsistency of critical theory and perhaps justifiably pointed dialectical thinking back in the direction of enlightenment.

Notes:

Habermas, Jurgen. *The Philosophical Discourse of Modernity: Twelve Lectures* (MIT Press: Cambridge, Mass, 1996).

Horkheimer, Max & Adorno, Theodor W. *The Dialectic of Enlightenment* (Stanford University Press: Stanford, CA, 2002).

1   Horkheimer, Max & Adorno, Theodor W. *The Dialectic of Enlightenment* (Stanford University Press: Stanford, CA, 2002), xviii.
2   Ibid., 1, xv.
3   Ibid., xviii.
4   Ibid., 4-5.
5   Ibid., 5.
6   Ibid., 7. It could be argued, though, that modern science also pursues ends through a type of mimesis. For example, Darwinist homologies between the human fetus and the human race appear to be very mimetic in their attempt to explain biological reality.
7   Ibid.
8   Ibid., 26-27.
9   Ibid., 34.
10 Habermas, Jurgen. *The Philosophical Discourse of Modernity: Twelve Lectures* (MIT Press: Cambridge, Mass, 1996), 106.
11 Ibid., 111.

12   Ibid., 113.

13   Ibid., 113.

14   Ibid., 114.

15   Ibid., 118.

16   Ibid., 118.

17   Ibid., 119.

18   Ibid., 119.

19   Ibid., 121.

20   Ibid., 123.

21   Ibid., 125.

22   Ibid., 130.

● CHAPTER 16 ●

The Art of War and Machiavellian Statecraft

The popular views attributed to fifteenth/sixteenth-century Italian diplomat and philosopher Niccolo Machiavelli are not actually his own. Having not actually read his works, many assume that he is known for advocating the notion that the ends justify any means while rulers of state must have no scruples in achieving their ends. While Machiavelli was a pragmatist in many respects, his positions place him firmly within the classical Western tradition of statecraft. Thinkers like Machiavelli during the Renaissance sought to revive classical Greek and Roman learning, and it is within that milieu that we must situate him. He did not advocate tyranny and abuse, and his insights on intrigue, subterfuge, and conspiracy illuminated and rebuked many of the errors of our degenerate, effeminate gaggle of so-called leaders. Machiavelli's political treatise *The Prince* is well known, but few are familiar with his *Art of War* and *The Discourses*, each of which contains a wealth of knowledge about the workings of the state and strategic designs, and it is to all of these we must look to gain deeper insight.

In *The Discourses*, Machiavelli described the cycle through which most civil states go, from oligarchy to revolution to democracy to anarchy. Revolutionaries should take note, as the "revolution" they often seek to inflame often ends up bringing an even worse tyranny to follow. Revolutionaries, unfortunately, are not historically known for a keen understanding of human nature, allowing their ideals to override the real, and as a result, the Marxist state, for example, found itself frustrated and collapsing from within. Add to this the fact that most historical revolutionaries have been the tools of foreign and economic interests, and we begin to see why the pattern persists. We can also see something akin to the future ideas of Oswald Spengler for whom patterns and cycles were crucial, timeless phenomena for historical analysis.

Machiavelli wrote of the cycle of the state in *The Discourses on Livy,* Book I:

> Having proposed to myself to treat of the kind of government established at Rome, and of the events that led to its perfection, I must at the beginning observe that some of the writers on politics distinguished three kinds of government, viz. the monarchical, the aristocratic, and the democratic; and maintain that the legislators of a people must choose from these three the one that seems to them most suitable. Other authors, wiser according to the opinion of many, count six kinds of governments, three of which are very bad, and three good in themselves, but so liable to be corrupted that they become absolutely bad. The three good ones are those which we have just named; the three bad ones result from the degradation of the other three, and each of them resembles its corresponding original, so that the transition from the one to the other is very easy. Thus monarchy becomes tyranny; aristocracy degenerates into oligarchy; and the popular government lapses readily into licentiousness. So that a legislator who gives to a

state which he founds, either of these three forms of government, constitutes it but for a brief time; for no precautions can prevent either one of the three that are reputed good, from degenerating into its opposite kind; so great are in these the attractions and resemblances between the good and the evil.[12]

We see here a realistic perspective inherited from the ancients. All governments are subject to corruption and tyranny, although some are more than others. The pattern for degeneration is monarchy becoming a tyranny, aristocracy becoming an oligarchy, and democracy becoming anarchy. This pattern also hearkens to Aristotle, who made a similar list in his *Politics*. History has seen many states, but all fall into these same basic forms. While some governments are certainly better in form than others, nothing can halt a corrupt, degenerate elite and populace from collapsing when moral degeneracy and corruption reign. However, there is an important realist corrective to modernity and progressive thinking here that cannot be passed over, which is that the reason for the collapse of any state is not the form of government itself, but the rise of corruption in the hearts of citizens. Modern liberalism, which is still the norm among most, in praxis at least, assumes that the solution to problems arises from changes in law and government. If we can only change our political leaders and get a new crop in! If we can only change the law to get proposition 666 passed, why, then we would have our freedom and progress! Nothing could be further from the truth, as the problem ultimately lies not in externals, but in people's own hearts. Corruption is rooted in and proceeds from individuals and their decisions, not from external forms and systems. Classical liberalism and modern liberalism are rooted in the metaphysical error of attributing the location of evil in some institution, and not in people's own decisions.

In this regard, Machiavelli was a pessimist with respect to human nature. While the Renaissance is often lauded for its high view of human nature adopted from the Greeks, Machiavelli did not see the populace as able to govern themselves. Heavily influenced by St. Augustine, Machiavelli developed a negative appraisal of human nature that placed him in a nondemocratic tradition of classical republicanism. While critical of monarchy because of its liability to fall into tyranny through its hereditary descendants, Machiavelli believed it was certainly not the worst form of government—democracy. Early seeds of the US Constitution can also be seen here, as Machiavelli is one of the most famous proponents of republicanism of the Italian tradition, and John Madison and Alexander Hamilton had clearly read and been influenced by the Florentine thinker, as *The Federalist Papers* appear to show. Elucidating the cycle of collapse, Machiavelli commented, with hints of the nascent social contract theory:

> Chance has given birth to these different kinds of governments amongst men; for at the beginning of the world the inhabitants were few in number, and lived for a time dispersed, like beasts. As the human race increased, the necessity for uniting themselves for defence made itself felt; the better to attain this object, they chose the strongest and most courageous from amongst themselves and placed him at their head, promising to obey him. Thence they began to know the good and the honest, and to distinguish them from the bad and vicious; for seeing a man injure his benefactor aroused at once two sentiments in every heart, hatred against the ingrate and love for the benefactor. They blamed the first, and on the contrary honored those the more who showed themselves grateful, for each felt that he in turn might be subject to a like wrong; and to prevent similar evils, they set to work to make laws, and to institute punishments for those who

contravened them. Such was the origin of justice. This caused them, when they had afterwards to choose a prince, neither to look to the strongest nor bravest, but to the wisest and most just. But when they began to make sovereignty hereditary and non-elective, the children quickly degenerated from their fathers; and, so far from trying to equal their virtues, they considered that a prince had nothing else to do than to excel all the rest in luxury, indulgence, and every other variety of pleasure. The prince consequently soon drew upon himself the general hatred. An object of hatred, he naturally felt fear; fear in turn dictated to him precautions and wrongs, and thus tyranny quickly developed itself. Such were the beginning and causes of disorders, conspiracies, and plots against the sovereigns, set on foot, not by the feeble and timid, but by those citizens who, surpassing the others in grandeur of soul, in wealth, and in courage, could not submit to the outrages and excesses of their princes.

Under such powerful leaders, the masses armed themselves against the tyrant, and, after having rid themselves of him, submitted to these chiefs as their liberators. These, abhorring the very name of prince, constituted themselves a new government; and at first, bearing in mind the past tyranny, they governed in strict accordance with the laws which they had established themselves; preferring public interests to their own, and to administer and protect with greatest care both public and private affairs. The children succeeded their fathers, and ignorant of the changes of fortune, having never experienced its reverses, and indisposed to remain content with

Jay Dyer

this civil equality, they in turn gave themselves up
to cupidity, ambition, libertinage, and violence,
and soon caused the aristocratic government to
degenerate into an oligarchic tyranny, regardless of
all civil rights. They soon, however, experienced the
same fate as the first tyrant; the people, disgusted
with their government, placed themselves at the
command of whoever was willing to attack them,
and this disposition soon produced an avenger, who
was sufficiently well seconded to destroy them.

The memory of the prince and the wrongs
committed by him being still fresh in their minds,
and having overthrown the oligarchy, the people
were not willing to return to the government of a
prince. A popular government was therefore resolved
upon, and it was so organized that the authority
should not again fall into the hands of a prince or a
small number of nobles. And as all governments are
at first looked up to with some degree of reverence,
the popular state also maintained itself for a time,
but which was never of long duration, and lasted
generally only about as long as the generation that
had established it; for it soon ran into that kind of
license which inflicts injury upon public as well as
private interests. Each individual only consulted his
own passions, and a thousand acts of injustice were
daily committed, so that, constrained by necessity,
or directed by the counsels of some good man, or
for the purpose of escaping from this anarchy, they
returned anew to the government of a prince, and
from this they generally lapsed again into anarchy,
step by step, in the same manner and from the same

causes as we have indicated. Such is the circle which all republics are destined to run through.[2]

The cycle of collapse for the republic is similar to that of the collapse of other forms of government, but it is all the more relevant for our present day. Since the French Revolution, the majority of the world's states operate under the auspices of being republics, but there is an important distinction to be made that Machiavelli could have never foreseen: global *shadow* government. In fact, it is Machiavellian realism that leads us to easily understand that our world is governed by international shadow entities that use nation-states as fronts. We are far beyond the outdated era of one nation-state going to war against a rival nation-state. Ours is the era of global oligarchical cartels in competition, with the Anglo-American establishment currently at the top. Cartels and empires have always existed, but the world has never seen a global secret technocratic shadow government, and in that respect, we are in a unique situation. The issues of corruption and degeneracy are not new, but they are more rampant than anything in Machiavelli's day precisely because there are newer, more sophisticated means of technological tyranny and evil than existed in any previous age. We can see from this classical perspective that conspiracies and espionage are not surprising—they are synonymous with perennial statecraft.

On conspiracies, Machiavelli explained in *The Prince*:

> But concerning his subjects, when affairs outside are disturbed he has only to fear that they will conspire secretly, from which a prince can easily secure himself by avoiding being hated and despised, and by keeping the people satisfied with him, which it is most necessary for him to accomplish, as I said above at length. And one of the most efficacious remedies that a prince can have against conspiracies

is not to be hated and despised by the people, for he who conspires against a prince always expects to please them by his removal; but when the conspirator can only look forward to offending them, he will not have the courage to take such a course, for the difficulties that confront a conspirator are infinite. And as experience shows, many have been the conspiracies, but few have been successful; because he who conspires cannot act alone, nor can he take a companion except from those whom he believes to be malcontents, and as soon as you have opened your mind to a malcontent you have given him the material with which to content himself, for by denouncing you he can look for every advantage; so that, seeing the gain from this course to be assured, and seeing the other to be doubtful and full of dangers, he must be a very rare friend, or a thoroughly obstinate enemy of the prince, to keep faith with you.

And, to reduce the matter into a small compass, I say that, on the side of the conspirator, there is nothing but fear, jealousy, prospect of punishment to terrify him; but on the side of the prince there is the majesty of the principality, the laws, the protection of friends and the state to defend him; so that, adding to all these things the popular goodwill, it is impossible that any one should be so rash as to conspire. For whereas in general the conspirator has to fear before the execution of his plot, in this case he has also to fear the sequel to the crime; because on account of it he has the people for an enemy, and thus cannot hope for any escape …

> For this reason I consider that a prince ought to
> reckon conspiracies of little account when his people
> hold him in esteem; but when it is hostile to him,
> and bears hatred toward him, he ought to fear
> everything and everybody. And well-ordered states
> and wise princes have taken every care not to drive
> the nobles to desperation, and to keep the people
> satisfied and contented, for this is one of the most
> important objects a prince can have.[3]

Here Machiavelli expounded the heart of conspiracy from the perspective of the ruler. Conspiracy need only be feared when the ruler is hated as a result of tyranny or sadistic cruelty. Fear is a crucial key in the arsenal of the state, but fear must be tempered by virtue and security, and the imbalance in either direction leads to sedition from others, and conspiracies become successful. For the ruler, the maintenance of goodwill among subjects is obtained through the management of public perception and genuine goodwill by the ruler. It is not a license for doing anything and everything to maintain power, something many wrongly accuse Machiavelli of doing; rather it serves as a balance of mercy and severity, and that power is maintained by fear. Contrary to popular opinion, Machiavelli firmly rebuked the notion of immorality and devious designs, opting instead for an approach of balance, with the ruler's reputation standing on its own through virtue. Any other imbalance leads the ruler to fall prey to his own vices and overthrown by his own self-destructive folly.

Roman Catholicism, through St. Augustine and classical virtue ethics, also factors into Machiavelli's tempering of the prince as it did for medieval warfare as a whole. This comes to the fore in his lesser-known *Art of War*, which was the first treatise on modern warfare that would revolutionize the field. For ancient and medieval leaders, the state, espionage, warfare and its deceptions, and the game of politics were considered "arts" that could be mastered only through study and practice. Systematizing everything—military camps, music, flags and colors, size and ranks—Machiavelli revolutionized the medieval army to become a hierarchical standard that would be the norm for future Europe. On another level, it also contains interesting aspects relating to psychological warfare, espionage, and deception that are instructive for us in our day that help to grasp the level of deception we live under. The ancient arts of statecraft and deception are not forgotten, they have been perfected and, through a high-tech overlay, are beyond anything Machiavelli could have imagined. He wrote:

> Birds or dust have often discovered the enemy, for where the enemy comes to meet you, he will always raise a great dust which will point out his coming to you. Thus often a Captain when he sees in a place whence he ought to pass, pigeons taking off and other birds flying about freely, circling and not setting, has recognized this to be the place of any enemy ambush, and knowing this has sent his forces forward, saving himself and injuring the enemy. As to the second case, being drawn into it (which our men call being drawn into a trap) you ought to look out not to believe readily those things that appear to be less reasonable than they should be: as would be (the case) if an enemy places some booty before you, you would believe that it to be (an act of) love, but would conceal deceit inside it.[4]

Book VI is the best section for these machinations, and in it we see the following perennial tactics:

- Consult a rising enemy or possible sedition to give the impression of heeding his ideas and win him by feigned interest.

- Send wise men into the enemy's camp as fake attendants of a fake dignitary to assess the enemy.
- Use false defectors to be spies in the enemy's camp.
- Conversely, capture the enemy's commanders to gain intelligence on the opponent.
- If you have suspected spies in your camp, disseminate false information to various parties to see how the enemy reacts to which.
- Sacrifice a town or some pawns as a gambit to give the enemy a false sense of security.
- Utilize religious and superstitious omens as far as your soldiers revere them or invent them.
- Disguise your soldiers as the enemy.
- Give the appearance of retreat to lead the enemy into a trap.
- Leave an open encampment for the enemy with fresh, albeit poisoned, supplies.
- Never cause an enemy to despair, since he will only fight more desperately and possibly defeat you.
- Use a subterfuge of a fake illness in your camp that leads the enemy to think you are weak.
- Communicate among your generals and men with secret ciphers and codes the enemy cannot decode.
- Use propaganda and stories to create a boost of morale among your men.

Many more could be listed, but these are the most interesting, and in our day, these tricks are used by the elite, not on foreign powers primarily, but as the bases for mass deception, with a massive surveillance state, poisoned food and water, false media reports, and countless other ruses. We might think from this list that Machiavelli was immoral and devious, but for him, these were necessary facts of war with the enemy, not with the populace itself. The goal of war for him was not virtue, but simply to win at all costs. Yet winning at all costs does not mean being sadistic or cruel or brutish; it means learning the art of war to be a just ruler, and by so doing, win the admiration of your soldiers and homeland. Far from being corrupt, Machiavelli castigated the corrupt leaders of his day, and this serves as an apt warning to ours. Corruption and effeminate degeneracy among the elite does not lead to power; it leads to the loss of power. As far as we concede to evil and vice in our own hearts, especially rulers, to that degree do we lose our power and become subservient to the passions.

Machiavelli concluded:

> But let us turn to the Italians, who, because they have not wise Princes, have not produced any good army; and because they did not have the necessity that the Spaniards had, have not undertaken it by themselves, so that they remain the shame of the world. And the people are not to blame, but their Princes are, who have been castigated, and by their ignorance have received a just punishment, ignominiously losing the State, (and) without any show of *virtu* …

> Our Italian Princes, before they tasted the blows of the ultramontane wars, believed it was enough for them to know what was written, think of a cautious reply, write a beautiful letter, show wit and promptness in his sayings and in his words, know how to weave a deception, ornament himself with gems and gold, sleep and eat with greater splendor than others, keep many lascivious persons around, conduct himself avariciously and haughtily toward his subjects, become rotten with idleness, hand out military ranks at his will, express contempt for anyone who may have demonstrated any

praiseworthy manner, want their words should be
the responses of oracles; nor were these little men
aware that they were preparing themselves to be the
prey of anyone who assaulted them.[5]

Notes:

1   Machiavelli, *The Discourses on Livy,* Book I
2   Machiavelli
3   Machiavelli, *The Prince*
4   Machiavelli, *The Art of War?*
5   Machiavelli

Printed in the United States
by Baker & Taylor Publisher Services